Inter-religious Dialogue

A SHORT INTRODUCTION

OTHER BOOKS IN THIS SERIES

RELATED TITLES PUBLISHED BY ONEWORLD

Inter-religious Dialogue

A SHORT INTRODUCTION

Martin Forward

ONEWORLD

OXFORD

INTER-RELIGIOUS DIALOGUE: A SHORT INTRODUCTION

Oneworld Publications
(Sales and Editorial)
185 Banbury Road
Oxford OX2 7AR
England
www.oneworld-publications.com

ISBN 1–85168–275–9

Cover design by Design Deluxe
Typeset by Saxon Graphics Ltd, Derby
Printed and bound in Britain by Bell & Bain Ltd, Glasgow

CONTENTS

ACKNOWLEDGEMENTS

I am extremely grateful to Novin Doostdar and Juliet Mabey for asking me to write this book, and to their colleagues at Oneworld for bringing it to birth. I am indebted to lots of people for the information and experiences that are offered here. Many authors and friends have guided me on the highways and byways of dialogue. I apologize for often failing to mention them or even to remember their precise influence.

I offer my particular appreciation to a number of people. Ursula King supervised my postgraduate work on the contribution of Geoffrey Parrinder to religious studies. I am extremely grateful to both for all I have learned from them, not only from their writings but also from their warm personal qualities. My friend Mohammed Alam has taught me a great deal about dialogue as friendship; I am grateful to him and to his family. I would also like to record my affectionate remembrances of my old colleagues at the Henry Martyn Institute, Hyderabad, India, where I worked from 1975 to 1977 and grew into a dialogical person: in particular, among others, Sam Bhajjan, Andreas and Diane D'Souza, Sisters Leelamma and Fatima, and David and Mary Lindell. I am also profoundly indebted to other friends whom I first met in India. I would like in particular to mention Anita Mukarji-Connolly. She may not agree with everything herein (who will?) but her deep passion for truth and justice, her committed friendship, her humour and courage, her troubling of me for the sake of truth and justice – these have been important to me over many years. The two women in my life, Udho and Naomi, have, as usual, borne my absences in the study almost too cheerfully!

I would like to dedicate this book to four dear friends. Kenneth Cracknell has been a mentor for well over twenty years. His contribution to interfaith dialogue has been outstanding. This book is for him and his equally distinguished wife, Susan White. To their names, I would join those of Jonathan Dean and Jane Leach. Kenneth and Susan, Jonathan and Jane have taught me so much about friendship as dialogue, and I am truly grateful.

INTRODUCTION

PERSPECTIVES

This book is complementary to my *Religion: A Beginner's Guide.* Whereas that book looks at the phenomenon or phenomena of religion, this one examines the possibility and desirability, even the absolute necessity, of positive relationships between people of different faiths. Although people of distinct religions have lived alongside each other for centuries, the modern world has added a special urgency to the need to do so respectfully and knowledgeably, since we now possess the means of destroying the whole created order. A somewhat hostile argument against religion would maintain that religious people have often marginalized and even killed those who think and act differently from them. A more positive case for religion would contend that, at its best, it has urged its proponents to deal justly and indeed tenderly with all people. At any rate, one hopes that respect for and knowledge of the 'other' will lead humankind away from the abyss. In our world of rapidly increasing modes of communication, not just a sense of survival but also the noblest impetuses of people of faith should lead them to understand, esteem and learn from others.

It may be useful to record the perspective from which I write. My father was a member of the Royal Air Force in the declining years of the British Empire. In 1957, I began my school years in Singapore. It took my family many days to get there by plane from Britain (the plane broke down on one occasion, giving us a delightful week in Brindisi, Italy), and a month to return by ship. Now, of course, the journey by plane to

Singapore is about thirteen hours, non-stop. There, I learned to associate fireworks with the Chinese New Year festival, rather than (as most British children do) with Guy Fawkes's attempt to blow up the Houses of Parliament in 1605. (That event had a religious component that most Britons have now forgotten: for many years, Bonfire Night on 5 November, celebrating the failure of Guy Fawkes's attempt to overthrow King James I, formed part of the myth of English identity; his effort was interpreted as a dastardly Roman Catholic plot against divinely sanctioned Protestant political authority.) I attended a Confucian wedding service before I remember going to church or Sunday school. Between the ages of nine and eleven, I was in Aden, that barren yet entrancing heap of sand at the heel of the Arabian peninsula. My father had been there twice before and introduced me to his friends of old. There, I began my lifelong fascination with Islam. Many years later, long after I began an academic study of the Muslim faith, my father told me that he had once been tempted to convert to Islam because of the many good people he had worked with who were Muslims.

At the age of twenty-three I went to India to be ordained deacon in the Church of South India and to be captivated by friends who were Christians, Jews, Jains, Hindus, Muslims or Parsees. Although I returned to Britain half a lifetime ago, in 1977, I go back to India as often as I can. It has become my second home: to quote the English poet, George Herbert, India is my 'land of spices ... something understood'. Now I find myself in my third home, Aurora, Illinois, close to the great city of Chicago and its rich multicultural and multi-faith mix of people.

My own religious pilgrimage is simply a rather extreme example of the possibilities that the twentieth and twenty-first centuries have opened up to many of the world's spiritual voyagers. We now have an ease of transport, rapidly expanding communications and technological networks, and other factors that point us towards a global culture. Yet we also witness, on our television sets, the dark products of such technology: the widespread poverty, warfare and death that afflict many members of the human family.

What role must faith and the faiths play in the new millennium? Some would say none, since religions have been and remain so destructive to many. Yet even in the secular West, religions flourish, if often in new rather than traditional forms. So it is foolish to ask whether we should have religion or religions. It is better to ask, 'What sort of religion or religions should we have?' The answer to this question will not arrive simply out of thinking profound thoughts, but from relationships. Dialogue is an essential strategy for meeting, understanding, valuing, learning and living together in peace.

As I have written in *Religion: A Beginner's Guide*, I am primarily a scholar of the relatively new discipline of religious studies. Although such intellectuals are often (though by no means always) practising members of a particular religion (I myself am an ordained Methodist minister), we attempt to understand and appreciate other ways of responding to the mystery of Transcendent grace that surpasses, but does not bypass, human insight and intellect. That is the perspective from where I stand. I am particularly grateful to and deeply influenced by the Christian tradition within which I have been nurtured and tutored. It has offered me a profound and challenging religious vision of and route through my life. Indeed, I am especially indebted to the Methodist inter-pretation of Christian faith, a point I shall return to later when I empha-size the importance of roots for – to coin a word – religious 'dialogicians'. We shall see that it is better to be a flower than a butter-fly. (Incidentally and whimsically, I prefer the term 'dialogician' to 'dialo-gian'. Both could be claimed to be analogical to 'theologian'. 'Dialogician' can also and usefully be compared with 'theoretician'. To be sure, theoretical and methodological issues are important to many of the concerns of inter-religious dialogue.)

My Christian perspective and background in the British inter-religious scene have strongly shaped the arguments in this text and the form they take. I make no apology for this. We must all start from some-where. We shall see that even those who assume an entirely objective perspective are conditioned by who they are and what they have learned; for good if they realize this; for ill if they mistake their perspective, however exalted they believe it be, for all that others see. This is true too of secularists. As we shall observe in Chapter 3, those who strive after the chimera of a scientific study of religion, freed from the constraints and supposed baleful influence of faith stances, search for fool's gold at the end of a rainbow. Although Christians have much to be ashamed of in their religion's condescension, arrogance and inflated sense of superi-ority, many Christians have been at the forefront of new discoveries and have shown wisdom and humility in their dealings with others. Still, if, for example, a Japanese Buddhist were to write this introduction, it would have quite a different feel. Nevertheless, since many Japanese Buddhists are deeply involved in inter-religious movements, there would be certain points in common, not least the conviction that religion, religions and religious people should be taken seriously in a world where secular people are often uncritically self-confident in the rightness of their points of view.

I hope readers will forgive those large parts of the text that are anecdotal and personal in style. On the one hand, dialogue is about the meeting of human beings who are willing to be honest and open with each other about important matters; disposed, in particular, to share aspects of the stories of their lives that intuit and illustrate the presence of Transcendent reality, and to listen eagerly to how Transcendence has graced other people. On the other hand, preachers and teachers who endlessly interpose themselves between their subject matter and their audience are excessively irritating. I have tried not to do so endlessly and egocentrically, but only when relevant and, hopefully, interesting.

INTENTION

My intention is to write a short introduction to inter-religious dialogue that will convince people that such dialogue is an enduring phenomenon, not one of the passing fancies of this age. I hope the book will prove useful to all who want to understand something of humankind's spiritual quest. Although that quest is 'conservative' in the best sense of 'conserving' from the past things that are of abiding value, faith must always be relevant to the present age. For this reason, dialogue is of significant importance for those who wish to live out their faith in the modern world.

As I intimate in *Religion: A Beginner's Guide*, I write with an enthusiast's zeal for his subject. When I spent my childhood in different parts of the world, observing the faith of Confucianists, Buddhists, Muslims and Jews before I ever heard of the Methodist form of Christianity that is now my home, I was entranced with the wonder of a child, which so many adults foolishly mistake for gullibility, by humankind's divergent expressions of the spiritual quest. I earnestly hope that some who read this book will be captivated by and drawn into the mystery of faith in relation to other faith.

What about the subject of faith? Christians call him (or her? or them?) 'God'. Others have different names for, and vastly different ways of connoting, a supra-natural reality to whose transforming presence this world is porous. Although I have used the word 'God' in this book, often that designation stands for the diversely conceived reality to which I have referred in the last sentence. Occasionally, as in *Religion: A Beginner's Guide*, I have employed the more inclusive designation 'Transcendence' or 'Transcendent reality'. The word 'faith' has also been the subject of much recent discussion. In some contexts the term 'faith' denotes the eager and willing, though sometimes misconceived response of human beings to the captivating allure of Transcendent reality. In other contexts it denotes one of the religions of the world – to provide a necessary change from endlessly writing the word 'religion'.

Chapter 1 asks, 'What Is Dialogue?' It contends that dialogue is not a trendy and ephemeral phase that will soon pass, but has an interesting and fruitful history. Chapter 2, 'Viewpoints in Dialogue', looks at the perspective from which people view faith. Chapter 3 ventures some suggestions about 'Dialogue in the New Millennium'. It argues for the cultivation of an interfaith theology of religions in the contemporary world. People of different faiths should together talk about the deepest things of faith and hope, not simply give their own religion's spin on these profound matters. We have much to learn from one another. It is indeed my conviction that religious people must work together in the modern world for the common good. In an era of globalization, it is no longer appropriate for us to act independently when we can work together. Chapter 4, 'To Mend the World', describes a particularly fraught and troubled relationship, that between Jews and Christians. It asks whether dialogue could achieve what confrontation cannot. It also alludes to other relationships, posing the question of whether the recent improvement in relations between Jews and Christians could be mirrored elsewhere. Chapter 5 is called 'Inter-religious Living in an Age of Globalization'. There are many contemporary issues that face the religions, like changing attitudes towards women and gay people, and ecological concerns. These will be examined in this chapter, which will end with a brief look at the desirability of an inter-religious and dialogical engagement with spirituality and truth.

MUNDANE MATTERS

Since this is a brief introduction to interfaith dialogue, I have kept notes to a minimum. In the text, I have sometimes, in brackets, pointed the reader to authors and to the dates of particularly relevant books by them, whose titles can be found by consulting the bibliography. The bibliography points interested readers to a selection of books that will take their exploration of religion further and deeper than I have attempted here. Wherever I have mentioned dates, the references are not to the various religious calendars but to before and after the Common Era. To be precise, dates in the text without a suffix are from the Common Era; if they precede the suffix 'BCE', this means the event they refer to was before the Common Era. Most religions have their own dating systems, but increasingly their members refer to their faith-specific calendars for internal use and employ Common Era dating in the public domain. Even though this system follows the Christian system of dating – though shorn of the confessional use of 'BC' (before Christ) and 'AD' (the year of the Lord) – it is widely used by scholars of religious studies.

I have already intimated that this book is complementary to my *Religion: A Beginner's Guide*, which I hope readers of this book will also acquire! However, I do not assume this to be the case. There is a small amount of common material between the books, though employed to different ends, and able to be easily understood by readers who examine only one of these works.

One last point. Religions are sometimes among the most sexist and hierarchical of institutions, although certain expressions of religion can be quite the opposite. (The origin of the word 'hierarchical' comes from one meaning 'priesthood'; some forms of religion see priests or their equivalent cultic or educational figures as superior beings to the 'laity', though most regard them as doing 'different' things and living out a 'different' or more 'concentrated' lifestyle than the laity; different, as opposed to superior.) In fact, some of the most exciting movements sweeping through contemporary religion are liberationist and egalitarian – though other religious people often resist them, occasionally for good reasons. I have tried to avoid sexist and other forms of exclusive language by using inclusive terms.

1 WHAT IS DIALOGUE?

DIALOGUE: A NEW PLAYER AT THE TABLE OF INTER-RELIGIOUS RELATIONS?

The Henry Martyn School of Islamic Studies was founded in Lahore, then part of British India (now in Pakistan), in 1930. It was named after the missionary Henry Martyn, and aimed to equip missionaries for evangelical proselytizing.

Martyn was a very distinguished missionary. He arrived in India in 1806. He translated the New Testament into Urdu, the *lingua franca* of Muslims in North India, and died in Persia in 1812, on the way back to England, carrying his Urdu New Testament and also unfinished scripts in Arabic and Persian. He was still a young man, little more than thirty years old. We shall return to Martyn later in this chapter, to examine his credentials as missionary and practitioner of dialogue. (I shall use the rather ugly word 'dialogician' to denote such a practitioner.) For the moment, it is important to note that the original ethos of the school was missionary, intending to convert followers of Muhammad into disciples of Christ.

The school's early staff members were extremely distinguished scholar-missionaries. Take, for example, L. Bevan Jones, a Baptist minister and the first principal of the school. His book, *The People of the Mosque*, first published in 1932, is, in the words of its subtitle, a well-informed 'Introduction to the Study of Islam with Special Reference to India'. It was written at the request of the National Christian Council for India – comprising clergy, pastors, evangelists, teachers and others – to help them deal with Muslim criticisms of Christianity and to address the concerns of converts from Islam. It is an impressive work. Bevan Jones had studied Islam for twenty years, and, given the parameters of his chosen audience, his book is a masterly survey of Islam and Muslims, entirely free from uncalled-for polemics. The chapter on 'A Candid Enquiry into Our Methods' reveals his conviction that Christians are called to be witnesses of the redeeming love of God in Christ Jesus, and maintains that Muslims are most impressed by the holy, Christ-like life.

When I went to work at the school, from 1975 to 1977, the ethos had changed. At independence, the school moved to India; finally, in 1971, it relocated in Hyderabad, a city that, though predominantly Hindu, had a strong Muslim minority and was deeply imbued with Muslim cultural values. The director was by then an Indian, Sam Bhajjan, a distinguished poet. I worked with two other Indian members of staff, Sisters Leelamma and Fatima, and with an American colleague, David Lindell. Before he went to Canada for doctoral studies, I met the man who, as I write, is the current director, Andreas D'Souza. I was not a missionary, but a fraternal worker. There were a number of reasons for this change: in those days, it meant that I did not need a worker's visa, but also it was intended to indicate that I was a junior colleague of Indians, not their master. Indeed, I was ordained deacon in the Church of South India.

Looking back, I can see that the school (which was by then called an 'institute', its name often shortened to 'HMI') was in a transitional phase. My colleagues used the word 'dialogue' rather more than the word 'mission', although, when pressed by me and others, found it difficult (as did I) to offer an easy definition of either term. A generous interpretation of this quandary would be that staff members of HMI promoted a healthy diverse approach to interfaith relationships, reflecting the great variety of Christian attitudes and actions to religious pluralism. But probably a truer estimate is that HMI was then uncertain about its *raison d'être*, and promoted events and an ethos that sent off different signals about its purpose. For example: staff members gave instruction about Islam to local clergy which was not quite polemical in tone but often rather unfriendly, and published material that was more combative than affirmative about other ways of faith. Yet we also held wonderful evenings at which people of different faiths would gather to celebrate each other's festivals, or read poetry together. Muslims, Hindus and other people of faith would often wander into the institute during office hours, to read newspapers or talk amicably to staff members.

So they felt mostly unthreatened and even at home in HMI.

One man, Hayath Khan by name, the imam of a mosque in a suburb of the city, taught me Arabic and took me home for Islam's high and holy days to share wonder, fun and friendship with his family. Whenever he talked of the mercies of Allah towards humankind, his eyes would fill with tears that would flow down his white beard; an impressive and touching sight. As I grew to know Arabic and more about Islam, he became fearful of my future state. Since I seemed respectful of Islam's claims but impervious to their calls upon me to change my religious allegiance, he was at a loss to know how to proceed. Should he teach me more, so as to gain my conversion to his religion; or give up instructing me, so that I would not suffer at God's hands for knowing too much and acting too little upon it? There was also the not trifling matter of my payment for his services. Religion is not simply about pious, uncontextualized faith. Hayath Khan was not well off, and the small amount I gave him for language tuition was a welcome addition to his income. So he was in a real dilemma. He continued to teach me, yet he found it more easy than I did or do to hold together notions of a good God who loves his human family but is willing to punish them mightily. Still, I remember him with thankfulness and great affection.

Since the 1980s, the focus of HMI has broadened to include the improvement of relationships between people of different faiths and traditions, and the encouragement of an objective and respectful knowledge of all religions, particularly Islam. This was seen to be a development of HMI's interests, not a betrayal of its foundation aims.

Currently, a particular emphasis is not just on dialogue, but on what the director calls 'dialogue in the slums'. After the destruction of a mosque at Ayodhya in October 1992 by some Hindus, who argued that it was on the birth site of Lord Rama, communal tension and even violence increased in many parts of India, including Hyderabad. HMI brought together a meeting of people of different faiths to decide what could be done to create peaceful relations among all communities. The group called itself the Aman-Shanti Forum: *aman* is Urdu (a language commonly used by Muslims) for 'peace', and *shanti* is Hindi (mostly a Hindu language) for the same concept. During times of violence, members of the forum help out in hospitals and in providing food for the needy. In more favourable times, the forum promotes skills-training centres in poor areas, bringing Hindus and Muslims together to work on common problems. Members speak in schools about their interpretation

of religion as a reconciling rather than divisive factor. HMI also continues to offer courses of study to improve knowledge of the 'other'. It
holds a summer course on Islam and interfaith relations, and offers a
master's degree in Islam. Students from all over the world come to the
institute to pursue guided reading – some from the seminary I used to
teach at in Cambridge, England, but many more from the USA, Canada,
the Philippines and many other countries.

Broadly speaking, then, one can distinguish three phases in the life
and work of the Henry Martyn School or Institute. The first was missionary in intention and proclamation; it could be claimed that this
lasted, more or less, until the move to Hyderabad in 1971. The second
was more equivocal, paying some rather vague attention to dialogue
while also maintaining a rather negative appraisal of Islam. The third
period, dating from about the mid 1980s onwards, has self-consciously
widened the participants to include Hindus and others and has been
more committed to social justice than theological and ideological disagreements.

Yet these three phases are not watertight. Bevan Jones was by no
means unappreciative of Islam; still less, of the lives of holy Muslims. In
my time, there were some, admittedly rather rudimentary, attempts to
work together for the common good. Current staff members are deeply
committed to Christian faith as well as to interfaith co-operation. Furthermore, although one can see a movement in HMI's ethos from
mission to dialogue, these words are still rather difficult to define. If,
right at the beginning of the school's existence, Bevan Jones was correct
to discern that Muslims are most impressed by holy Christian living,
who is to say that, in working together with Christians for the common
good, Muslims might not be so impressed that they turn to Christ?
However, what Bevan Jones failed to see, or perhaps to admit, is that
these matters work both ways: Christians might be so impressed by a
goodly and godly Muslim that they turn to a Muslim way of faith.

HMI's growing interest in dialogue rather than mission raises the
issue of whether the two terms are mutually incompatible: dialogue
rather than mission? In fact, this may be a false or at least overstated
antithesis. Since, as I have suggested, the three phases of HMI's history
are not watertight, the many attempts to define 'dialogue' in absolute
distinction from terms like 'mission', and to see the two ideas as utterly
incompatible may be misconceived and doomed to failure.

DIALOGUE: A DEFINITION

How rooted is dialogue in the long history of human faith upon earth? HMI lighted upon the term, in a serious way, in the 1970s. This makes historical sense, because in Protestant Christian churches dialogue took off as an officially endorsed stance towards people of other religions in the 1970s, a little later than in the Roman Catholic Church. Although the reforms of the Second Vatican Council had encouraged Catholics to view people of other faith with charity and in esteem since at least the publication of *Nostra Aetate* in 1965, the major Orthodox and Protestant ecumenical instrument, the World Council of Churches (WCC), had dragged its feet. Figures like the Dutchman Visser t'Hooft and the Briton Lesslie Newbigin, though no doubt impressive for other things, had imbibed the cautious and negative theology of Karl Barth and Hendrik Kraemer towards the faith of other people, and insisted that only exclusive and introvert beliefs should be served up to member churches.

Finally, in 1971, a Sub-unit on Dialogue with People of Living Faith and Ideologies was founded within the World Council of Churches, under the direction of Stanley Samartha and later Wesley Ariarajah. This sub-unit soon promoted guidelines that were actively endorsed by many of its member churches.[1] These guidelines were:

- Dialogue begins when people meet.
- Dialogue depends upon mutual understanding and mutual trust.
- Dialogue makes it possible to share in service.
- Dialogue becomes the medium of authentic witness.

Within Christian faith, this emphasis upon dialogue could look puzzling, and actually did so to many very suspicious members of the WCC's committees. Words like 'mission' and 'evangelism' have a long pedigree in Christian history, but 'dialogue' looked like a newcomer to the table, an alien intruder and not an old and trusty friend. Is this so?

We can start to answer this question by attempting a definition of 'dialogue'. We should begin by recognizing that there is now a flourishing industry examining how language functions. It has become evident (though not always to scriptural exegetes, who still pore over every word) that to examine the linguistic origins of every word and to draw minute and detailed conclusions from them can be a very dubious enterprise. Nevertheless, though noting this warning, it is salutary, instructive, and may even gain us some credibility, if we pause to reflect on the word 'dialogue'.

Some contrast it with 'monologue', as though dialogicians listen and learn out of respect for other viewpoints, rather than simply and solely talk and offer their own point of view. No doubt this form of dialogue is estimable, but, if we are brave enough to venture into linguistic origins, it will become doubtful whether 'monologue' is the exact opposite of 'dialogue', as can be seen from looking at the structure of the word 'dialogue'. The second part of it comes from the Greek *logos*, meaning 'word' but having a variety of cognate meanings, including a worldview or a coherent principle of how things are. Thus the opening of John's Gospel, hearkening back to the very beginning of the Bible, which tells us that God created the heavens and the earth by speaking, informs us that 'In the beginning was the *logos*'. There are many shades of meaning here, including the idea of a word as a spoken utterance, and as a rational and coherent principle of the universe: these meanings become flesh in Jesus (John 1:14).

What, however, of the first part of the word 'dialogue'? It is 'dia-', not 'di-' as many people wrongly infer. In Greek, 'di-' indicates 'two' rather than the 'one' that is signified by 'mono-'. But 'dia-' is a preposition that means 'through'. '*Di*-logue' could mean *two* people conversing about a worldview; maybe amicably, maybe not; maybe with results, maybe not. But '*dia*-logue' signifies worldviews being argued *through* to significant and potentially transformative conclusions, for one or more participants. It involves a much more consequential encounter.

Since language experts have warned us not to be too pedantic in our interpretations of how language functions, let us not press this too far. Instead, let us take a brief look at good and bad things associated with di-logue and dia-logue. The danger of inconsequential dialogue, di-logue, is that sometimes it is rather gushy, arising out of manufactured or rather comfortable and unchallenging situations. I call this the 'more tea, vicar?' sort of rendezvous. On the other hand, dia-logue, arguing important matters through to conclusions, has its problems too. It can easily fall into a traditional view of asserting your own position, without being challenged by the other. Yet I prefer dia-logue to di-logue. It recognizes the importance that religious people attach to their own particular stance. It may be that the conclusions they argue for will be modified or even changed in the context of listening to others. It stresses dynamism, process, means and ends, so is radical and not easeful and sheltered. This interpretation of dialogue allows it to be challenging and open ended. Participants are risk takers because they themselves learn and change; dialogue does not allow them just to inform and hope to transform others. They are aware that the process of their engagement with the 'other' provides space for Transcendence to make his or her or its or their presence available to all who participate in the enterprise of dialogue.

If this interpretation has any validity, then, although the word 'dialogue' may be relatively new in the vocabulary of inter-religious engagement, the attitude behind it is longstanding. There have been many distinguished human practitioners of dialogue in history.

The rest of this chapter will look at individual dialogicians from different times and homes within the worlds of religion. One of them, Socrates, could be labelled an intellectual; another, Paul, was a religious leader, though far from a conventional one; a third, Akbar, was a politician; the fourth, Sri Sarada Devi, was an ordinary, even uneducated young woman, until she became seen as an aspect of the divine mother. Sometimes the interfaith movement has wanted to marginalize politicians as enemies, or has appeared to be the preserve of official spokesmen (usually men, and occasionally self-appointed as officially endorsed) or of academics, rather than of ordinary people. My chosen list of people illustrates that dialogue can and ought to be undertaken by a wide variety of people at several levels of faithful human living. After discussing past individual dialogicians, it will look at the developing inter-religious movement, addressing Britain as a particular example. Finally, it will ponder what these extraordinary individuals have to tell people in the modern or post-modern world about creative inter-religious engagement. In particular, we shall have to ask whether their extraordinary quality is a sign of their marginality and even alienation from proper and fundamental faith commitment. Or are they pioneers of a better way?

But first, we need to look at the word 'inter-religious' – or rather, at the word 'religion', which lies behind it. In Chapter 1 of *Religion: A Beginner's Guide*, I raise the contentious matter of defining religion. The comments that I discuss in this paragraph are discussed there at greater length. Briefly: there is much contemporary debate among scholars about whether religions, defined as boundaried systems of beliefs and practice, actually exist or else are a creation of recent Western and, ironically, secular history. At the time of the Treaty of Westphalia in 1648, which brought to an end the Thirty Years War in Europe, the Latin world *religio* was given a meaning that it originally lacked. That treaty defined the Roman Catholics and Protestants each as a separate *religio*, thus marking an important stage in making that word a generic term for all organized religious communities. The roots of that definition lay earlier, in the sixteenth-century Reformation, and its flowering was in the designation of diverse though interconnected Indian traditional religions as a unitary Hinduism by nineteenth-century Western orientalists. In medieval times *religio* meant a state of life bound by monastic vows, and was never used for the particular aggregations of cultures and beliefs that are now called Hinduism, Judaism, Buddhism, Christianity and the like. Arguably, Europeans have been obsessed with categorizing and reifying diverse phenomena. Thus, Hinduism, Christianity and the 'religions' of the world are vastly more pluriform phenomena than has usually been noticed in the recent past. This debate has usefully enabled us to see that religions are more open ended than we might have supposed, and that their adherents not so uniform in thought and action.[2] Even so, it is foolish to overstate the problems surrounding the concept of religions as boundaried systems. Ludwig Wittgenstein's notion of 'family resemblances' is helpful on this point.[3] As it is applied to religions, one could say that there is no essence of religion which all religions must possess to be classified as such. Rather, there are resemblances between them that constitute them as religions and, so long as each religion possesses certain of these likenesses, then it stands as a religion. This means that religions are bound to be phenomena that have fuzzy boundaries.

It also means that it is proper and useful to make comparisons between religions to locate similarities and differences, just as one might draw comparisons between how different family members look and behave. So, as a Methodist Christian I might have more in common with a Tibetan Buddhist than with another Methodist Christian. In fact, I am absolutely certain that I do have more in common with my Tibetan Buddhist friend Dorji than I do with many people on the countless Methodist and ecumenical church committees I have served, or with whom I have worshipped on a Sunday morning! His openness to other points of view, humour, kindness and suspicion of the value of committees are not the prerogative of Christians, nor, at least in practice, even treasured by all of them.

Once I grant this internal diversity with yet certain common characteristics within religions, I am committed to the notion that whatever it is I wish to share with others in dialogue, even if I profoundly disagree with them, it is not the certain conviction that they should become part of a rigid and monolithic Methodist form of Christianity. Even so, most religious people have assumed that it is important to be rooted in a particular tradition or some part of it, rather than to subscribe to a more eclectic and personal religiosity. Although such figures as the Emperor Akbar (as we shall see) raise a question mark against this point of view, I have much sympathy with it. So, in the next chapter, I shall write about the importance of roots for people engaged in dialogue, and develop this topic there.

It is easy and, to some extent, justifiable to use the terms 'interreligious' and 'interfaith' interchangably. Still, the towering figure of Wilfred Cantwell Smith has cautioned us against this. For him, faith is, at least potentially, a universal human quality of openness towards Transcendent reality. This should be a warning to those religious people who think that they alone, through the religious system they embrace, have the ability or even the capacity to respond to ultimate reality. John Bowker has raised the possibility that humans are genetically prepared for religion by dint of the capacity for faith in that which is greater than sentient reality.[4]

SOCRATES, THE GADFLY OF WESTERN PHILOSOPHY

Let us begin our brief survey of important practitioners of dialogue, in ancient Greece. Socrates did not establish Western philosophy, but he certainly transformed it. There is remarkable agreement that philosophy began in the half millennium or so after 800 BCE. This period witnessed the work of Confucius and Lao-Tse in China, the Buddha in India, the prophets in Israel, Zoroaster in Persia, and Homer and the philosophers in Greece. Some have called this the 'axial age', since the axis of world history seems to have changed during this long period of time. Before it, even great civilizations like that of Egypt were pre-philosophical. After it, more reflective societies grew up: in Israel, India, China and Greece.

Socrates lived from 470 to 399 BCE, about half-way through this axial age, in Athens. We know him through the writings of his disciples, Xenophon (c. 430–354 BCE) and Plato (428–354 BCE). Socrates was ugly, poorly dressed, barefoot, and argued in the marketplace about the just, the true and the good. Humans sin, in his view, through lack of knowledge. Knowledge is virtue, and the major cause of evil is ignorance. This is a debatable standpoint, but Socrates would no doubt have enjoyed arguing the case with any who disagreed with him, since his method of enquiry was as important to him as the decisions that were reached thereby. In short, his dialectical method was that of question and answer. He was not sceptical about truth, but believed that it could be drawn, little by little, from his partner in this process. Although the terms 'dialectical' and 'dialogical' are not synonymous, one can argue that Socrates' use of question and answer was a form of dialogue, drawing knowledge and insight out of the other. One hopes that, like all good teachers, he learned from that process too and from his pupils' wrestling with knowledge and meaning.

In the Enlightenment West, philosophy and theology, reason and religion have often been divorced from each other, rather than held in a creative relationship. Not so, elsewhere. In India, although there have been atheistic strands of teaching, philosophy has not usually wished to deny Transcendent reality but rather has insisted upon the importance of the role of human reason in interpreting encounters between humans and supra-human reality; similarly, Islamic philosophy has held together belief in a revealed God with a place for human thinking and deduction, and has proved decisively important for Muslims, despite the reservations of many conservative interpreters of religious law. Thus, in south and west Asia, Transcendent reality and human beings are often interpreted as in a dialogical process of mutual debate and interaction.

How religious was Socrates? In the modern and post-modern Western world, many have seen Socrates as the father of sceptics. Looking at the list of philosophers from the axial age, one might distinguish those who were religious (the prophets of Israel and Zoroaster) from those who were not (most of the rest). But this would be a false contention. I have pointed out in *Religion: A Beginner's Guide* that the Buddha and Confucius, although they were sceptical about the power of a creator God to save, nevertheless believed that there is more to life than meets the eye, and that it is necessary for humans to discern what that 'more' is and to give their lives to following its meaning for them and for all. So there is little reason to dub Socrates an atheist, unless you have personal reasons for wishing to read him in that way.

Like many foundational religious figures, Socrates tantalizes us by leaving us no written word of his beliefs. In the vein of Confucius, he seems to have been chary about committing himself to any coherent view of human post-mortem existence. Perhaps he believed in the migration of the soul at death, or perhaps not. Also like Confucius, and the Buddha, he seems to have been far more interested in how to be virtuous in the here and now than to speculate futilely about the future. Still, he seems to have been logically persuaded that individuals were either the product of blind chance or else of intelligent design, and to have plumped for the second position, with its concomitant belief in a God who is extraordinarily knowing and powerful.

Socrates was not a popular man. Like a number of philosophers since, he was politically naïve. Although the oracle at Delphi called him the 'wisest man in Greece', it overlooked his political ineptitude. He was friendly to some of the 'Thirty Tyrants', who executed many of their Athenian opponents. It was for that reason, as much as for his supposed corruption of young men by his ideas, that he was condemned to death. Still, he worried the old and the powerful by his extraordinary capacity to influence outstanding young men with new and exciting ideas: he troubled them with truth. Xenophon was a general, and Plato the scion of an aristocratic family. Socrates was brought to trial in 399 BCE. There, he uttered probably his most famous maxim: 'the unexamined life is not worth living'. He thought that most of his contemporaries spent their lives chasing fame or riches or pleasure without ever questioning the importance of these ephemeral things. If they continued in this way, they would never be able to know if they were doing the right thing, and might misspend their lives. No wonder he was popular among certain idealistic figures but a dangerous gadfly to the minds of many more. His dialogical method led him to his death by execution. The cup of hemlock that took away Socrates' life is a salutary reminder that dialogue can be a troubling and dangerous enterprise, raising absolutely crucial questions that many people would desperately wish to remain locked away in the recesses of the mind, undreamed and unexamined.

We owe much that is important in Western (indeed, in human) thought to this man and to his extraordinary influence upon his disciples; above all, upon Plato. Alfred Whitehead (1861–1947) observed that 'the safest general characterization of the European philosophical tradition is that it consists of a series of footnotes to Plato'.[5] If so, then Socrates is of truly outstanding importance.

Perhaps it could be claimed that, whereas Socrates and his followers assumed and sought a single thread of reason and logic, much inter-religious dialogue has been a more bewildering involvement in issues to do with the authority and mutual engagement of truth systems, each claiming validation by Transcendent reality. To be sure, Socrates lived in a less complicated, though still pluralistic world. However, the Socratic *process* of dialogue is of particular significance for religious dialogicians.

Socrates' commitment to a process of question and answer set up a dialectical method that has been of importance to many philosophers since. Let us consider one example of his method. In Plato's *The Republic*, Socrates questions Cephalus, Polemarchus and others to elicit from them a true account of the nature of justice. Cephalus suggests that justice means 'telling the truth and paying one's debts'. Socrates points out that if you borrow a weapon from a friend who then goes mad and demands it back, you would not feel it appropriate or just to hand back the weapon. This insight leads to the need to produce a new definition of justice which will include both the original contention and the contrary case. It could be argued that the method is an early example of Hegelian dialectic (Hegel lived from 1770 to 1831), in which the thesis produces an antithesis and both resolve in a synthesis. This points to the element of truth in Whitehead's maxim that later Western philosophy merely developed Platonic insights. More to the point, it shows how precisely open to the truth as an exploration humans should be. Truth is located through (dia-) a dynamic process and is not accessible as a static given.

Religious people (though not just religious people) are often bad at allowing the truth to be open ended. Sometimes they refer to the Bible or Qur'an, to past precedent or the teaching of the guru as a sufficient reason for interpreting truth as a clear-cut entity, like a particular medicine to be applied to wounded humans for their instant cure. We shall return to this partial and closed view in Chapter 5, to illustrate its flaws. For the moment, it is crucially important to point out that the search for virtue, for truth, is liberative when it is explored, elicited, examined; not when it is inferred or imposed. To take one foundational religious example: according to John's Gospel (3:21, 8:38), Jesus talked of doing the truth, and that the truth will be known and would set free its knower; this presupposes a dynamic process, not an imposed, authoritarian revealed commandment.

Jesus and Socrates are not so far apart, after all. What a pity so many religious Christians do not get this point. Until recently, I worked for almost six years in a seminary where students aged from twenty-five to fifty-five trained for ordained Christian ministry. The best of them were engaged with the search for truth, wherever it took them. Yet the less able saw truth as a skill to be mastered, not a quest to be discovered. The former group are dialogicians, open to explore the awkward meanings of life. The latter are potentially low-level thought police, interested in imposing stark and often meaningless simplicities on themselves and on others. The former breathe the spirit of Socrates of Athens, as well as of Jesus of Nazareth and many other figures who are open to the mystery of a Transcendent reality to which this world is porous.

Plato's resort to élite guardians who controlled reason in his ideal republic, modelled more on the severe Spartan society than on his own Athens, shows how even enormously important followers of great men can, to some extent, betray the latter's ideals.

PAUL, CHRISTIAN (AND JEWISH?) APOSTLE TO THE GENTILES

For almost two hundred years, some scholars (latterly including Jews and Muslims, as well as eccentric Christians) have argued that, just as Plato misunderstood crucial aspects of Socrates, so the apostle Paul unwittingly betrayed the simple gospel of Jesus.[6] Well, Jesus' good news about God was perhaps not so simplistic as some have inferred. Moreover, as we shall see in this section, Paul was closer to Socratic dialogue than to Platonic imposed idealism.

An interesting task for a Christian is to be asked to talk to a group of Jews on the festival day of the Conversion of St Paul (25 January). You may be told that Paul was a renegade Jew; and that he betrayed the simple faith of Jesus for a complicated and Hellenized religion, and was thus the founder of Trinitarian Christianity. If you mount a modest defence of the man, you might just win the admission that, however misplaced his views of Judaism, he certainly argued like a rabbi.

Paul was indeed a very Jewish thinker. Even so, his passionate commitment to Jesus as the Messiah, the Son of God who fulfilled the Jewish Torah, teaching that included the Religious Law, and opened God's covenant mercies to gentiles as well as Jews, meant that he was far from being a mainstream Jew. No wonder, then, that at best most Jews have seen him as irrelevant to Judaism; at worst, as we shall see in Chapter 4, they have execrated him as the founder of a gentile movement that has seen itself as replacing Jews, who have no right to continue their existence as Jews.

Many Christians misunderstand Paul to have converted from Judaism to Christianity. It is a modern, Western view of faith to see it in such self-contained, boundaried ways. In fact, Paul always saw himself as a Jew. When he was arrested for taking a gentile into the inner court of the Temple, his defence before the Jewish court of the Sanhedrin consisted in a declaration that he was a Pharisee, a particular sort of Jew (Acts 23:6). His action was admittedly an eccentric thing for a Jew to do but not a piece of Christian point scoring on Paul's part; rather, it was an illustration of his passionate belief that God's promises were now open to gentiles as well as, not instead of, Jews.

Just as many mainstream Jews ever since Paul's day have seen him as misguided, so he regarded his co-religionists' failure to recognize Jesus as the Messiah, the agent of God for the salvation of all, as, to say the least, deeply mistaken and problematic. In his letter to followers of Christ in Rome (written about the mid to late 50s of the first century), chapters 9–11 lament this conviction. This short passage is full of emotion and contradictions. The Christian scholar Ed Sanders has noted that Romans 9–11 makes seven bewilderingly varied assertions: 1) despite appearances, God is just; 2) Israel was elect and remains so; 3) the election was selective and never covered every descendant of Abraham; 4) Israel, at least at present, has stumbled; 5) God will save only those who have faith in Christ; 6) all Israel will be saved; 7) everyone and everything will be saved.[7] This is a mystifyingly unsystematic, incoherent set of assertions. Paul was a passionate man; but his passion could not quite square the circle of his insight that God was, in Christ, reconciling the world to himself with his immense passion that Jews would be saved as Jews, according to God's promises.

It may be that Paul can be claimed as, in his own estimation, always and forever Jewish, though so alien to most other Jews that he remains, in their view, either renegade or bizarrely strange to the point of making himself an outsider. Whatever: it seems odd to claim him as a dialogician. Yet it is worth making the attempt.

There is a stereotype of tourists who never stay in one place long enough to benefit from the sights and sites, but chalk everything down to experience, buy the T-shirt and move on to the next encounter. Hence the supposed saying of such a tourist on holiday in Europe: 'If it's Tuesday, it must be Belgium.' It is easy but misguided to depict Paul as the Jewish or Christian religious version of this; a kind of first-century tourist. On this view, he wandered around the eastern Mediterranean, founding Christian churches and then moving swiftly on. Close attention to the New Testament book of Acts and to his own writings gives the lie to this interpretation. He stayed long enough in many areas to build up an impressive group of contacts and close friends. In fact, Paul sought to establish groups of Jewish and gentile believers in Jesus as the final agent of God.

In each place, he went first to the synagogue. Only when he was rejected there did he concentrate on teaching the gentiles. Furthermore, he stayed surprisingly long in each place (or so it seems to a son of a member of the Royal Air Force; in my childhood, we moved sometimes three times each year, and never stayed anywhere for much over two years).

Take Paul's stay in Ephesus, recorded in Acts 19. About the late summer of 52, Paul made his way to Ephesus, in western Asia Minor; today, on the Turkish coast, south of Izmir. The book of Acts records this as a time of great opportunity for Paul, but also a time when he faced many adversaries. Upon his arrival he found about twelve 'disciples', possibly followers of John the Baptist, whom he baptized in the name of Jesus. He then entered the synagogue, where for three months he spoke about the kingdom of God. Then he removed to the lecture hall of one Tyrannus, where, for a period of two years, perhaps from about 11 a.m. to 4 p.m. each day, he engaged in public debate. (This is the record of the western text of Acts, different at points from the version in the New Testament, but certainly a credible account of this incident.) We are told that Paul healed people, and converted numbers of those who had practised magic arts. Just as he resolved to leave the city, Paul fell foul of the president of the guild of silversmiths, Demetrius by name. According to Acts, the guild made a lot of money out of fashioning miniature images of the goddess Artemis. Paul's success at persuading some of her erstwhile worshippers to join the Jesus movement led to a riot stirred up by Demetrius. The silversmiths and others raised the cry 'Great is Artemis of the Ephesians', artfully linking the goddess to a sense of civic identity. They manhandled two of Paul's associates; Paul himself had to be persuaded not to go and try to appease the crowd. A certain Alexander seems to have tried to defend his people, the Jews, to the crowd, by dissociating them from the apostle's work but they saw he was a Jew, like Paul, and cried out all the more. Eventually, the town clerk quieted the crowd, arguing that matters should be resolved with due process of law; he would have been mindful of his responsibility to the Roman colonial authorities for the maintenance of public order. Thereafter, Paul soon left Ephesus.

At first glance, Paul's visit to Ephesus hardly looks like either a success story or the triumph of dialogue over more violent religious stances. But aspects of the story merit careful attention for practitioners of dialogue, and to these we now turn.

It is intriguing that Paul lasted for three months in the synagogue, arguing his case there. The words used in Acts 19:8 about his teaching method are often translated along the lines of him 'lecturing' and 'persuading' Jews about the kingdom of God. The first Greek word used is *dialogomenos*; close to the English word 'dialogue'. It could be argued that it involves a relaxed or overstated view of how language functions to deduce from this that Paul was involved in dialogue in the synagogue. But there are grounds for thinking that he must have been. If he had merely preached, or spoken and not listened, he would surely not have lasted two hours, let alone three months. In fact, all Jews believed in God's kingdom. There was much common ground between all people at the synagogue and Paul, though most Jews would have drawn the line at his presentation of Jesus as the Messiah who brought in God's kingly rule. So it is likely that Jews were at first intrigued to hear Paul's claims about Jesus, though eventually most wished to reject them, eject him and get on with their religious lives. Even so, according to Acts, it was not the synagogue authorities but some unidentified individuals who 'were stubborn and disbelieved, speaking evil of the Way before the congregation' (19:9; RSV). Furthermore, when Paul moved his centre of activity to the hall of Tyrannus, he no doubt employed the debating methods of Greek philosophers to attract and interest new gentile recruits, as well as to edify older followers, just as he had done at the Areopagus in Athens on a one-off occasion (Acts 17:22–34). So there is reason to believe that Paul conformed his method of presenting his good news to the style his different audiences were used to; but also, that he listened and pondered as well as urged and challenged.

Paul was not apologetic about his message. With some pardonable exaggeration, the author of Acts wrote that Paul's methods in Ephesus ensured that all residents of Asia (by which the writer meant, roughly, modern Turkey) heard the word of the Lord, whether Jew or gentile. Yet Paul trusted enough in his own faith not to shout down another's, and he believed that his message built upon his hearers' authentic prior encounters with God. No doubt, he believed that the message of God's dealing with his human children in Jesus should transform the knowledge of God or the gods that his audience had already experienced; yet his good news was no bolt from the blue to people who otherwise would have known nothing of the demands of Transcendence upon their lives.

The violent end to Paul's stay in Ephesus does not negate its witness to Paul as a dialogician. Certainly, that uprising helps to underline the fact that the practice of dialogue is no sentimental swapping of insights that have no real value or consequence for people. No less than Socrates, Paul was a troubler for the sake of truth; he, too, died for his vision. Like many dialogicians, Paul has been a much misunderstood man. His aims and motives have been trivialized. His willingness to listen and learn have been downplayed. He has been claimed by some as a villain, a betrayer; by others, as a proclaimer of exclusive certainties who would brook no other point of view than his own; by yet more, as a misogynist and muddier of clear teaching that he unnecessarily complicated. Paul was a much more complicated and interesting person than his opponents or even many of his supporters have supposed.

AKBAR AND GOD

The Mughal Emperor Akbar ruled North India from 1556 to 1605. Born a Muslim, Akbar exhibited a remarkable tolerance towards other religions. In mid-life, he created his own religion, the *Din-I-Ilahi*, with tenets that included: prayer three time a day; vegetarianism; *karma* and rebirth; kindly discourse towards others; and compassion to all living creatures. It is possible to see influences from Hinduism, Jainism and Buddhism, perhaps even more than Islam, in this amalgam of beliefs and practices. Akbar debated with scholars from other faiths, often chairing the meetings himself. He talked with Jains and Sikhs, and summoned Taoist and Confucian scholars from China. In 1578, he sent to Goa for representatives of Christianity. He adopted certain Hindu practices: he celebrated the festival of Dipavali, drank water from the Ganges and wore the *tilak* (a sacred mark on the forehead) and sometimes the sacred thread of the brahmin caste. He would also wear a Parsi girdle, and prostrate himself before the sun as Parsis did.

Was this new religion a denial of Akbar's birth faith of Islam? Certainly, he defied or ignored important Islamic laws. He married Hindu wives, and did not insist that they convert to Islam. He abolished the *jizya*, or poll tax on monotheists. He allowed Hindu converts to Islam to revert to Hinduism if they wished, justifying this by the Qur'anic teaching 'Let there be no compulsion in religion' (2:256). Most eccentrically, his new interpretation of religion gave himself a starring role. He possibly adapted Muslim mystical teachings about the perfect man to refer to himself. His coins were stamped '*Allahu Akbar*', the conventional Muslim utterance that 'God is greater'; yet this could also be interpreted to mean 'Akbar is God'.

So: was Akbar a dialogician, a dilettante or a despot? Perhaps he exhibits elements of all three, though he was mostly a despot. The fact that he was an enlightened and successful one, if also startlingly egocentric, indicates that his religious convictions were at least in part taken to ease his control over the foreign lands he ruled. His family was from Muslim Iran, not from largely Hindu India. If Muslim law were to be imposed on Hindus and others, that could signal the beginning of the end of Mughal rule by fomenting dissidence and discord; his less astute successors were to discover that fact. Muslim law may have required him to tax non-Muslim believers in one God and to seek the conversion of all others; Akbar knew that would be political madness. He was certainly no madman himself, so, if he did indeed encourage others to see him as the perfect man, he was no doubt acting in his own political interests: subjects who regard their ruler as perfect, or even as God, do not easily rebel against him, and, if they do, can be dealt with summarily as wicked and impious.

Was Akbar simply a cynical politician? Certainly, there has been a long tradition of rulers who have employed religious imagery to buttress their power and have persuaded people of faith to connive at their actions. The thirteenth-century BCE Egyptian Pharaoh Rameses II depicted his power in wonderful style at Abu Simbel, showing himself towering like a physical giant over his enemies. Of course this was self-serving; but it was more than this. Most of his subjects would have been grateful for a great and long-lived ruler who kept foreign enemies at bay, and would have believed, as Rameses himself did, that he fulfilled the will of the gods, of whom he was the earthly representation. Why not? Theirs was not an unworthy or foolish conviction. Despots with an eye to the usefulness of religion for political ends can also be pious, and even dialogicians and dilettantes. Many of the Hebrew Bible's Psalms also extol the king as God's representative, even his son. This furnishes a further example of the political dimension of religion. Yet many kings of Judah and Israel were no doubt devout as well as despotic.

A wholly sceptical interpreter of Akbar's actions could no doubt read all he did as the actions of an astute autocrat, determined to keep himself in power. Yet there are grounds for thinking that he was a truly, if unconventionally, religious man. He supported Hindu cultural practices, but also clamped down on actions like *sati* (the burning of widows) which he considered unjust, even if his deeds made him unpopular with sections of the Hindu community.

As to whether Akbar was a renegade or apostate Muslim, we should note Marshall Hodgson's astute judgement:

> The universalist sort of culture and moral life which Akbar fostered, and which was largely accepted as the basis for court life by Muslim and Hindu officials alike, was not in itself inconsistent with Islam. Indeed, it was cast in Islamic terms, and attracted its most explicit support chiefly among Muslims rather than among Hindus. But it presupposed an alternative interpretation of Islam, as it bore on life and culture, which excluded the more particularistic, communalistic, interpretation of the Islamic mission in the world which had always been upheld by the Shari'ah minded.[8]

Who determines true faith is a question that faces every dialogician, since they often stand at the edge of or even outside the boundaries set by guardians of orthodoxy and orthopraxy. No doubt it is a good thing that even kings have to answer to prophets. Even so, religions are susceptible to multiple interpretations: *intra*-faith as well as *inter*-faith dialogue is a necessary and inevitable process.

It may seem misguided or even absurd to include Akbar as a dialogician. But he is a useful reminder that dialogue is to do with more than personal faith. If dialogue is to make sense at all, it must make sense of religion as a focus and motivator for the common good in the political arena, not just for individual piety or sectarian advantage. One might criticize Akbar for many things but he does illustrate this fact well.

SRI SARADA DEVI

Thus far, my examples of dialogicians have been men. All of them have been public figures and, in many societies, the public arena has been open only to men until very recently. In some places, it still is. 'A woman's place is in the home' has been the maxim in most cultures and religions. This has raised issues, at least in the late modern and post-modern world, that we shall discuss later in this section and also in Chapter 5. Still, women have been and remain no less religious than men; probably more so, in fact.

Let us take Sri Sarada Devi (1853–1920) as an example. She was married to Ramakrishna (1834–1886), who, named Gadadhar Chatterji, was born into a poor Brahman family at Kamarpukur, Bengal, in northeast India. It was an arranged marriage: Sarada was five years old when they were betrothed, and her husband was twenty-three. Ramakrishna became an ascetic (their marriage was never consummated), and had visions of the goddess Kali, and also of other religious figures, including the Buddha and Jesus Christ. He taught that all religions were paths to the same goal.

Ramakrishna came to believe that, after his death, his widow would act as a spiritual teacher, so he taught her about the unsubstantial nature of the world, and its sorrows. He urged her to cultivate detachment from transitory things and grow in devotion to God, who alone is real and everlasting. This could seem a typical piece of masculine browbeating. But the following story may indicate that, having helped her accomplish all she could be, he then learned from her.

The day for the worship of the Divine Mother was 5 June 1872. At 9 p.m. Ramakrishna sent for Sarada, and sat her upon the special seat meant for the Deity. Then he began to worship her with flowers and offerings, uttering the mantras intended for the worship of Sodashi, the Divine Mother revealed as a sixteen-year-old virgin. At the close of worship, both Ramakrishna and Sarada were transported to the other-worldly plane. Then, as the culmination of his long years of spiritual practice, Ramakrishna offered himself completely to the Divine Mother revealed in the person of Sarada, and surrendered to her his rosary, all he possessed and himself. Thereafter, until the end of his life, she served him, cooking for him and for his disciples. Later, she described these as the best years of her life, for she was able to serve him and watch him sing and dance ecstatically.

After Ramakrishna's death from cancer, Sarada Devi was about to take off her ornaments, the custom of Hindu widows, but was prevented from doing so by a vision of her husband, who told her that he had simply moved from one room to another. Most of the rest of her life was spent at Jayrambatu, her birthplace in west Bengal, or in Calcutta. Sarada remained a guide and inspiration of the new Ramakrishna Order, founded in 1897 by Swami Vivekananda, which developed along twin paths of spiritual development and social service. She was known by devotees as 'the Mother', and is honoured as an avatar (a 'down-coming' of the god).

The emphasis in Ramakrishna's teaching upon the unity of all religious experience was not lost upon his widow. At a time when caste Hindus spurned outcastes or untouchables, she regularly addressed one such, Ambika, a village watchman, as 'brother'. Once, he told her that he did not understand why she was called a goddess, the Divine Mother and other names. She told him that he did not have to understand: 'Just remember that you are my brother Ambika and I am your sister Sarada.' Another story tells of how Amjad, a Muslim robber, built a wall for her house, and was invited for a meal. Nalini, Sarada's niece, threw the food from afar at Amjad's plate. Sarada admonished her and waited upon him; then she cleaned his plate herself when he had finished his meal. Nalini was shocked, and told her aunt she had lost her caste. 'Keep quiet,' Sarada said. Then she added, 'As Sarat [a disciple] is my son, exactly so is Amjad.'[9]

A cynic could suggest that men have duped women into accepting inappropriate and servile roles, and that religion has been the means of this oppression. In this view, religion is primarily a mechanism of social control by men over women, and not mainly a means of being open to the impact of Transcendent grace and goodness. So, the honour given to Sarada was essentially on men's terms and aimed to fulfil their vision of reality. She was essentially more circumscribed and less fulfilled than ideally she could have been.

It is true that men have used religion, explicitly or implicitly, to allot to women roles that they might not have chosen for themselves. However, there are reasons to suppose that religion has sometimes enabled some women to subvert these roles. Some women have lived lives so transparent to Transcendence, as their disciples interpret it, that they have become exemplary figures, to some extent breaking the bonds of conventional, patriarchal assumptions about what they should be and do. Not only Sarada but also the Muslim Rabia of Basra, the Christian Julian of Norwich and many other women saints and mystics illustrate this point.

What Sarada and many other such women illustrate is the importance of internal resources and external constraints upon religious dialogicians. The constraints within which women live their lives are often narrower than those open to men. (Even so, all humans are boundaried by social, economic, religious, linguistic, educational and other considerations.) Indeed, it could be said that, despite the example of her generous attitude towards people other than caste Hindus, Sarada had very little to do with dialogue as we know it. She lived within external constraints largely imposed by men, even as they venerated her. Nevertheless, within these constraints, she lived a life of piercing goodness and intuitive insight into Transcendent grace and goodness. Furthermore, the internal resources of her faith that all religions were paths to Transcendence provided her with an active generosity towards others when occasions arose in which she could so easily have practised conventional religious and cultural apartheid.

THE CONTEMPORARY INTERFAITH MOVEMENT

Rather than looking at specific individuals in more recent times who have promoted dialogue, I shall give a brief overview of the contemporary interfaith movement. However, it would be perfectly possible to look in detail at certain dialogical figures. I co-edited a book for Kenneth Cracknell's sixty-fifth birthday in 2000.[10] He was the first executive director of the British Council of Churches Committee for Relations with People of Other Faiths. Most of the book's contributors are Christian, for the emphasis of the work was upon Professor Cracknell's encouragement to Christians to live dialogically in our multi-faith world. The book has twenty-five contributors, and at its end a list of over eighty people who sent their greetings. It would easily have been possible to produce a similar *festschrift* made up of many of Cracknell's associates from the wider world of faith outside Christianity. All these people are dialogicians. Troublers for truth like Socrates, Paul, Akbar and Sri Sarada Devi are not confined to the past as pious ancestors to be venerated. We should not foolishly mourn that they have no present progeny. Their offspring are numerous and growing.

The modern interfaith movement perhaps began with the Parliament of the World's Religions held in 1893 as part of the four hundredth anniversary of the coming of Columbus to the New World. On 11 September that year, the Columbian Liberty Bell at the World's Columbian Exhibition sounded ten times, symbolizing what were then esteemed as the ten great religious traditions: Hinduism, Buddhism, Jainism, Zoroastrianism, Taoism, Confucianism, Shintoism, Judaism, Christianity and Islam. Nowadays, others would jostle to join that list. The great primal faiths of the world would be among them, and adherents of one of its important components, the Native American religions, would have strong words to say about an event associated with such a problematic historical event as the coming of white men with their exclusive ways, not least their exclusive religion. Other criticisms can be made of that parliament and its successors, including one that took place a hundred years later in 1993. A Briton like me, who treasures his country's history, not least its claim to be home of the 'mother of parliaments', is not inclined to take kindly to a group of self-appointed, often rather dilettante people, appropriating that term for their activities. Moreover, Islam was hardly represented at the parliament in 1893. Still, it was a remarkable achievement, despite such criticisms. Women were strongly represented, and there was a strong social aspect to the debates (as well as a number of expected if wearisome rose-tinted apologetics for the religion of some speakers who criticized others' faith, interpreted in negative ways).

The 1893 parliament was, in some ways, more impressive than its successor of a century later. It also contrasts with movements towards ecumenism within the Protestant churches at the end of the nineteenth century. There, certain groups and individuals were talking of 'the evangelization of the world in our generation'. John Mott's book of 1900, *The Evangelization of the World in This Generation*, popularized this slogan. (Mott, an American Methodist layman, who was to be important in Christian ecumenical work, was in other respects a remarkable Christian man.) This motto seems more a reflection of overconfident people at the high noon of empire than an accurate reflection of the teachings of the founder of their religion, who had valued the faith of a Samaritan, a Roman soldier and a Syro-Phoenician woman.

The most important figure of the 1893 parliament was not a Christian but a Hindu, Swami Vivekananda (1862–1902), whom we have already met as the chief disciple of Ramakrishna. (Before he sailed for the USA, he sought Sarada's permission, which was gladly given. She told him, 'Come back safely after conquering the world. May the Goddess of Wisdom dwell on your tongue.'[11] His message of the truth of all religions proved attractive then and since. Many South Asians have been at the forefront of dialogue in the twentieth century, though in recent years another, more intolerant, strand of Hindu tradition has been gaining ground. It would be possible and fruitful to chart the history of dialogue in South Asia, but I shall turn now, for another example of the growing mood towards dialogue, to the responses of the Western Christian churches.

In recent years individual Christians and even churches have been at the forefront of improving inter-religious relations. It is fascinating to speculate why this should be. Christians have too often been destructive of others' cultures and worldviews, so one cannot use the pioneering role of Christians as an indication of that religion's superiority over other faiths. Indeed, most Christians involved in the inter-religious movement would not usually be so boastful or naïvely confident about the absolute and unique truth of their faith. In some cases, their contribution has been facilitated by the fact that Christians hold considerable power and so can influence the course of inter-religious dialogues. In Chapter 4 we shall see that the poisonous Christian history of anti-Semitism has led individuals and churches to pioneer new relationships with Jews in the post-Holocaust world. Christian faith, in its recent Western forms, has been strongly influenced by, but has also strongly directed and even created, movements towards freedoms of speech and worship and the establishment of other human rights. Of course, these examples are double-edged. Many Christians have been deeply committed to issues of justice and peace, but Christian history and even present Christian practice have often been lamentable in their response to diversity.

The inter-religious movement in the United Kingdom is a particular example of which I have some knowledge. Britain has always been a land of immigrants, and the twentieth century saw the arrival of many members of other religions. I offer two generalized examples. In the 1930s, Jews arrived fleeing from Hitler's rule and joined their co-religionists in London, Manchester, Leeds and elsewhere. After World War II, South Asian Muslims, Hindus and Sikhs from the newly independent countries of India and Pakistan, later joined by South Asians from East Africa, came to Britain in large numbers. So-called 'coloured' immigration provoked the Conservative politician Enoch Powell's infamous 'rivers of blood' speech in April 1968, when he predicted large-scale racial conflict in Britain unless the tide of immigration was not merely stemmed but reversed.

Many Caribbean and other immigrants have been or are Christians. But it became clear by the 1970s in Britain that the days when the churches dealt with other faiths by sending missionaries abroad to meet their representatives were over. The cultural and religious landscape of the land was changing, so that, for example, you could converse in the Scottish island of Stornaway with a Scot of South Asian descent in Urdu or Gaelic rather than in English.

It was time for a more positive, dialogical interaction of people of different faith in Britain. The 1973 oil crisis, when the price of petrol was raised enormously by Middle Eastern suppliers, led some Christians to want to understand better the world of Islam, if only for reasons of *realpolitik*. (It has taken the British churches a long time to realize further that there are several forms of Islam to be discovered. That religion is not a monolithic phenomenon, usually depicted as fundamentalist and hostile to Western priorities.)

Christian responses to the presence of people of other religions in Britain in the 1970s did not arise *de novo*. For some time, Britain had produced a number of eccentrics who had ventured into relationships with people of other faiths. Sometimes their oddity, or the imperial context in which they operated, or other factors, led them into false positions. For example, Sir Richard Burton's pilgrimage to Mecca in 1853 mired him in deception, in that he masqueraded as an Arab Muslim in order to fulfil the conditions of the *hajj* (the pilgrimage to Mecca and Medina in the sacred month, which all Muslims hope to make once in their lifetime; these holy areas are forbidden to non-Muslims). Burton's admiration and contempt for the other (and, if one were a psychiatrist, one might be tempted to add, for himself) were in unresolved tension. One could make much the same case for a man like T.E. Lawrence (of Arabia). Yet Lawrence's more eminent soldier-successor in west Asia, Sir John Glubb (Glubb Pasha), who wrote that 'I am happy to be a Christian, but I have also loved Muslims',[12] is an extraordinarily attractive figure, whose biography of the Prophet Muhammad is full of sound judgement, wise choices and spiritual discernment. Rather a fantastic figure was Sir Francis Younghusband, the subject of a splendid biography,[13] whose creative interpretation of Christian faith led him to found the World Congress of Faiths in 1936,[14] one of the first of many (perhaps too many) interfaith movements that have sprung up, often out of the British situation or else the result of a Briton's brainwave. Their recent successors are people who have spent much time in multicultural areas for the sake of Christian love and ministry, when often they could earn better salaries or enjoy a more comfortable lifestyle elsewhere. There are many such people. One might note Roger and Pat Hooker's distinguished Christian presence in the English Midlands area of Smethwick. Upon Roger's untimely death, many friends of Christian and other faith paid tribute to this distinguished Christian scholar and gentleman.

The word 'dialogue' began to be used around the 1960s, as local interfaith groups grew up in cities and towns across the United Kingdom. Many depended upon the extraordinary commitment of individual Christians: Stella Reekie inspired Glasgow's Sharing of Faith group; Peter Bell was inspirational in Leeds's Concord; and Ivy Gutridge devotedly led the Wolverhampton Interfaith Group. Other local interfaith groups, though well meaning, were less impressive and gathered together like-minded conversationalists whose desire was to prattle rather than to act. It was painful, in Leicester in 1985, to have to help found a Council of Faiths, whose founder members had found it difficult, indeed impossible, to work with the local interfaith group.

It may be interesting to record briefly the origins of the Leicester Council of Faiths, of which I was the first joint-secretary. After her Sikh bodyguards killed the Indian Prime Minister Indira Gandhi, in October 1984, there was much tension between Leicester Sikhs and Hindus. A local police official suggested to David Silk, then Archdeacon of Leicester, and a number of other leaders and representatives of the religions of the city that it would be good for them to meet together on a regular basis to diffuse tension. So we did.

One amusing incident occurred at that time. In the tenth century, a group of Danes ravaged central England and killed the Bishop of Leicester. Absent-mindedly, the English church forgot to replace him until 1937. In 1987, Robert Runcie, the Archbishop of Canterbury, was invited to lead the celebrations of the fiftieth anniversary of the Diocese of Leicester's refoundation. A few weeks before the celebrations, Nathubhai Jagjivan phoned me. He was President of the National Council of Hindu Temples (UK) and the leader of the large local Hindu temple, Shree Sanatan Mandir (formerly the William Carey Memorial Baptist Church). He asked me if I could persuade Dr Runcie to visit the temple while on his official visit to Leicester. Although I had no particular access to his grace of Canterbury's ear, I knew a man who did. I phoned David Silk and put this request to him. 'Leave it to me', was his reply. I did; and he came up trumps. The Archbishop agreed to come. Ten days before Dr Runcie's arrival, Nathubhai phoned me again.

'Martin, this will be the first official visit by an Archbishop of Canterbury to a Hindu temple. I want to make a speech of welcome that won't embarrass him or us. Please have it on my desk tomorrow morning.'

So I did. About three days later, the phone went. It was the Archbishop's secretary, calling from Lambeth Palace.

'Mr Forward,' she said, 'Dr Runcie's visiting the Leicester Hindu temple shortly. He's anxious to say warm and affirming things, but nothing that will cause offence to his hosts or to ordinary church members. Please will you write something appropriate and let me have it tomorrow.'

So I did. A few days later, I sat with my wife Udho in Shree Sanatan Mandir and listened to the President of the National Council of Hindu Temples (UK) and the Primate of All England read out my speeches.

Getting to know people of other faith certainly does enlarge one's horizons and one's experiences, and contributes to life's fun and fullness. A decade or so ago, Archbishop Trevor Huddlestone came to give the major speech at the opening of the Leicester Jain Temple, formerly a United Reformed church, and then the only Jain temple in the Western world. He talked about the goodwill and good deeds of the creator God, in whom Jains do not believe. But the Archbishop's gracious presence made him a most acceptable master of ceremonies, and people listened raptly and contentedly to him. Interfaith friendships not only help people indulge others' foibles and forgive their ignorance, but, more important, they enable people to work together for the common good. Over the years since its foundation the Leicester Council of Faiths has had a great deal of influence in social matters, such as the appropriate religious education of children in schools (this is a compulsory subject in British schools, though it is often badly done – except when schools are encouraged and enabled to speak appropriately to the children in the communities they serve).

Christians have taken a leading role in local interfaith groups. In the 1960s and 1970s, some churches established community projects to help immigrant communities, including those of other faiths. I was minister of one such church in Leicester and chair of its community project from 1984 to 1988. Looking back, I believe that there has been an unresolved tension in many such situations: a tension between social responsibility and theology. Our care for others, if it is not to become patronizing and if it is to discern when it is no longer necessary in its current form, needs to be built upon an adequate understanding of God's relationship to and acceptance of all his human family. Often, in the British scene, theology has lagged behind the desire to do something for the perceived needy. This seems all right, but it is not. Our actions are influenced by our understanding of the sort of God that God is. If, in our view, he is patronizing, or interested only in a person's economic welfare, we shall convey that impression. If God loves because that is his will and his nature and his delight, so shall we.

Brian Pearce has been an enormously important person in the British interfaith scene. He took early retirement from a senior post in the civil service to pursue a personal interest in interfaith relations. He set up the Inter Faith Network of the United Kingdom in 1988, which has listened to and brought together local interfaith groups, provided some thought-provoking publications, and which regularly brings together faith community leaders to meet, eat and converse together. In 2000, Pearce was honoured with the Papal Award Knighthood of St Gregory. The network links over eighty-five bodies and intends to make Britain a place marked by mutual understanding and respect between religions, where all can practise their faith with integrity. Its way of working is based on the principle that dialogue and co-operation can prosper only if they are rooted in respectful relationships that do not blur or undermine the distinctiveness of different religious traditions.

One other important area in furthering good interfaith relations in the United Kingdom, and elsewhere, ought not to be overlooked: that of religious broadcasting. Under Pauline Webb's leadership, the BBC's World Service Religion programmes for radio began to represent more widely not only the United Kingdom's but the world's religious diversity. Her successor, David Craig, though a committed Anglican, was even more insistent that the Religion Department was not a Christian chaplaincy. He worked to produce quality programmes on a wide range of faith issues and to open up theological reflection and even worship on air to the members and the concerns of a wide range of faith traditions.

I sometimes think that the churches' work in the area of Britain's religious pluralism began to falter just at the point when other faiths and broadcasting began to react seriously to contemporary British society. To some extent this is unfair. Much good work was done in the 1990s and still is being done. Yet financial constraints have not helped. We have already met the commanding figure of Kenneth Cracknell, appointed in 1978 as the first executive director of the British Council of Churches (BCC) Committee for Relations with People of Other Faiths. In 1992 the BCC gave way to the Council of Churches of Britain and Ireland and a full-time secretary of a Committee was replaced by a part-time secretary of a Commission. I doubt that the trade-off of name for time was a good one, though Christopher Lamb did sterling work in the post. His successor and the present incumbent of the half-time Church of England and half-time ecumenical post is Michael Ipgrave, a priest in the Diocese of Leicester who has good links with Japan. It remains significant that many people who take seriously the situation of religious pluralism have had knowledge of other cultures and languages. This is a particular problem in the United Kingdom (maybe especially in England), where some still seem to think that the world of untrustworthy foreigners begins at Calais.

The good work that has been done over the last quarter of a century has coincided with a deepening decline in the British churches' influence in society and in their active membership. This has led some critics to sneer that interfaith activities have been a diversionary tactic to persuade participants that all is not as bad as it seems. On this view, cuddling up to people of other faiths simply illustrates the bankruptcy of British Christians, who are attracted to other worldviews but cannot sustain interest in the one they have inherited. Nothing could be further from the truth. In his time at the BCC, Kenneth Cracknell began a journal called *Discernment*. It seems to me that panic has led many British church leaders to manage decline by emphasizing skills. Some even provide a theology for justifying the management of decline. In this they are guilty of enacting a self-fulfilling prophecy: if you manage decline you will manage to achieve it. The results can be seen in British theological colleges today (though not only there!), where the weaker students endlessly want to be taught skills or techniques of management: how to hold a baby at a baptism; how to stand at a funeral service; how to manage a pastoral visit; how to chair a meeting. At best these are of secondary import. More important are things like intuition, empathy, flair, interest in the needs of others at least as much as in one's own fulfilment – in a word, discernment. These categories are common in the wider world of interfaith relations, though sadly missing from the ghettos of many Christian institutions and among their leaders. At a time of decline in British churches, Christians engaged in interfaith relationships have pointed to a better way than skills and management: to the apostle Paul's belief that Christians must embody God's love for all his human children. This is not some foolish attempt to quench the Spirit by mechanisms of control and containment. It has to do with the renewal of God's work, not its decline.

THE INTERFAITH WORLD SINCE HENRY MARTYN

I began this chapter by referring to the Christian missionary Henry Martyn. We seem to have come a long way from his views. It would be easy to present this as a move from rejection of others' cherished beliefs to a respectful acceptance of them as alternative ways of belief and practice. But let us pause on Martyn for a moment to illustrate the fact that realities are more complex and interesting than this plausible caricature.

Martyn went to India as a chaplain to the East India Company. The British authorities in South Asia knew that disturbing the religious beliefs of Indians would not aid their control of the subcontinent. Clergymen were tolerated as chaplains to European workers, but were not encouraged to disturb, still less attack, the faith of Hindus, Muslims, Sikhs and others. Shortly before Martyn went to India, the directors of the East India Company had minuted the view that 'the sending of missionaries into our eastern possessions is the maddest, most extravagant and most unwarrantable project ... ever proposed by an enthusiastic lunatic'.[15] So, like all early missionaries to India (certainly before the Charter Act of 1813 and, in practice, for some years thereafter), Martyn was not free to espouse the form of mission associated nowadays with certain revivalist preachers in the USA and elsewhere, who mock other points of view from a narrow, and often superficial and repellent, one of their own.

Not that he would have wanted to condemn another's religion; rather, his instinct was to commend what he believed his own had done for him, and could do for others also. Certainly, he wished to offer Christ to the people of India. In a sermon in 1807, he said, 'How marvellously is India put into the hands of a Christian nation for a short time – may we lay a lasting foundation for the gospel in it.'[16] But, for Martyn, that gospel was not an invitation to fear God, nor was it a triumphalist assertion of Western cultural values. Rather, he made it clear that to be a Christian

> is not to have been born in a Christian country and of Christian parents; to have received the sacramental ordinances of baptism and the Lord's supper; and to live a moral and honest life; but it is to be in Christ ... a state very different in nature and importance from the mere external possession of Christian privileges, or the importance of relative duties.[17]

This passage causes the reader to wonder where Martyn's capacity for friendship and openness to others might have taken him had he lived longer. Perhaps this somewhat mystical, personal relationship with Transcendent reality might have led him to see it clearly in others, mediated through the 'external' forms of another religion.

All human beings are creatures of their own time and space, and reflect the pride and prejudice, the hopes and the glories of their particular and specific circumstances. Nevertheless, dialogicians are often at their most interesting when they break through the boundaries, to new possibilities.

So we move, in Chapters 2 and 3, to a discussion of appropriate theologies for dialogical people, which can enable them to break through to a view of Transcendent reality that envisages him, her, it or them as loving all that Transcendence has created, not just a part of it.

2 VIEWPOINTS IN DIALOGUE

Arnold Toynbee's twelve-volume *A Study of History*,[1] marvellous survey though it is, raises an important issue. His review of past times implies that he himself is an outsider to the ebb and flow, changes and chances, of the human enterprise, magisterially commenting upon it. Yet no human being has that impartial and detached perspective upon history. All of us are caught up in the processes of living and dying, seeing what we can from where we are, and (in many cases) living by its light. Iron-ically, Toynbee's book looks dated now; its gracious tone and ambitious theorizing reflect very much the tarnished certainties and the fretful worries of Great Britain towards the end of its age of imperialism.

Much recent theology of religion reflects the same mood. An edgy lack of confidence underlies its universalizing certainties. This chapter begins by looking at and criticizing its most popular form. Then it asks what are appropriate alternative strategies for a dialogical theology of religion. It explores my own Methodist resources for dialogue as an illus-tration of how every dialogician might examine their own religious resources to work out how to live faithfully in a religiously diverse world. Finally, it makes some practical suggestions.

EXCLUSIVISM, INCLUSIVISM OR PLURALISM: OR NONE OF THESE?

Many Christian theologians contend that a relevant Christian theology of religions, which takes the fact of religious pluralism seriously, is urgently needed in the contemporary world. They believe that we are living through a period when there has been a significant 'paradigm shift'. The term is borrowed from the philosopher of science Thomas Kuhn.[2] He argued that there comes a point when new information about a scientific subject or area forces scientists to give up old models and find new ones to describe how things now look. As applied by theologians to the world of diverse faiths, the concept of a paradigm shift acknowledges that our knowledge about other faiths can no longer be contained within old theories. What is needed is a new theology, or view of Transcendence, that will cope more adequately with the facts of experience.

Such a theology was put forward with particular clarity in Alan Race's book *Christians and Religious Pluralism*, first published in 1983. The subtitle drew attention to 'Patterns in the Christian Theology of Religions'. There are three: exclusivism; inclusivism; and pluralism. To put these patterns at their simplest: the exclusivist maintains that salvation is given only to those who make an explicit commitment to Jesus Christ; the inclusivist affirms that salvation is bestowed on others besides Christians, because of all that God has done through Jesus Christ; and the pluralist affirms that humans are saved within their own faith traditions, not (except for Christians) because of the person or works of Jesus.

It has been pluralists who have led this debate, and others who have responded to it. Naturally so, since pluralists are in the vanguard of those who wish for a paradigm shift, away from traditional notions of salvation and Christology, to more tolerant and open-ended attitudes towards the other.

Arguably, the most distinguished and influential of contemporary pluralists is John Hick. He argues, from an astronomical analogy, that the old paradigm placed Christ at the centre of the religious universe; though often, in practice, Christianity substituted for him:

> The traditional dogma has been that Christianity is the centre of the universe of faiths, with all other religions seen as revolving at various removes around the revelation in Christ and being graded according to their nearness to or distance from it. But during the last hundred years or so we have been making new observations and have realized that there is deep devotion to God, true sainthood, and deep spiritual life within these other religions.[3]

So what is needed is a Copernican revolution in Christian attitudes towards other faiths. The findings of Copernicus transformed the Ptolemaic map of the universe, so that people thereafter knew that the earth was not the centre of things, but that it and the other planets revolved around the sun. Now we need a paradigm shift to place Transcendent reality, however named, whether personal or non-personal, at the centre. Christian faith, or even Jesus himself, is not at the centre of things. According to Hick, like other, equally true religions, Christianity is contingent upon God, is blessed by him and witnesses to him. A telling illustration of Hick's shift of direction is the change of tone and title, though not so much the substance, of one of his early books. *Christianity at the Centre* was published in 1968; then it became *The Centre of Christianity* in 1977; in 1983, an edition was called *The Second Christianity*. The strong impression is that this second Christianity would be less self-centred, more tolerant of other ways of faith, and would witness to God's presence in the world rather than its own exclusive importance in his strategy of saving humans from sin and from hell. Hick dismisses the idea of a single world religion as unlikely to be achieved, and undesirable because some religions will always interpret ultimate reality as personal whereas others will define it as non-personal. So he would like to see them act in respectful ways towards each other, and to recognize that each is an equally acceptable mode of channelling Transcendence to those who seek more to life than meets the eye.

Hick's has been a liberating view for many thoughtful Western Christians who have been aware of and shamed by Christianity's condescending and even destructive history towards other religious groups; for example, towards Jews in medieval and modern Europe, and the first peoples of the Americas. They observe that many of their co-religionists are no better, and sometimes seem a great deal worse, than members of other faiths. Even so, such Christians might have a twinge of doubt about aspects of the pluralist approach. It is an ideological interpretation, moving beyond the simple, obviously true fact that there are many religions on earth, to a commitment to the conviction that such variety is a good and creative thing.

One of the shrewdest criticisms of Hick has agreed with him that God has many names, but has found him wanting in defining what distinguishes true from false views of Transcendence.[4] Geoffrey Parrinder discerned that same point many years ago. He wrote that

> The Pluralist position is ... unsatisfactory if it is taken to mean that all religions are the same, which they clearly are not, or that it does not matter what people believe. Questions of truth and goodness are important. The religion of the ancient Aztecs, who held up the beating

hearts of their victims to the sun, was clearly not so good a faith as the peaceful way of the Buddha.[5]

Quite so. We could add that such judgements can be made within as well as between religions. The teachings of the peaceful Buddha have been sullied by some violent and exclusive attitudes by, for example, a few Buddhists in Sri Lanka towards Hindus and Christians who share their land. Some missionary methods in Christianity have not cohered with the teachings of Jesus about loving God and other people. Such examples could be drawn from all the world's religions.

Pluralists tend to emphasize a history of Christian exclusivism. Hick's books often mention the Council of Florence (1438–1445). It defined the axiom *extra ecclesiam nulla salus* (no salvation outside the church) to mean that all those outside the church are excluded from salvation. This was officially the Roman Catholic Church's teaching until the reforms of the Second Vatican Council (1961–1965). Yet pluralists do not always mention that the Council of Florence was directed at medieval fissures within Christendom as much as at the wider world of other religions.

Indeed, one example of Western cultural parochialism is its emphasis upon salvation, which may be more Protestant than Catholic in its emphasis. Catholics tend to have a stronger belief in a natural theology than do Protestants; one in which the gifts of nature and not just supernatural events can demonstrate God's presence in the world. Protestants tend to overemphasize both.

Joe DiNoia, a Roman Catholic priest and scholar, has noted that 'prevailing positions in the field of theology of religions for the most part focus their energies on allowing for the possibility of salvation outside the ambit of Christianity'.[6] Hick, a compelling exponent of such a position, is a Protestant who has moved from a naïve fundamentalism to a belief that all religions are more or less equally valid paths to salvation or liberation. He has strengthened his newer conviction by drawing on the philosopher Immanuel Kant's distinction between noumenal and phenomenal; the 'thing-in-itself' and its perception. That is: truth exists as it really is, but is also appropriated, to be sure in fragmentary fashion, within cultural contexts in ways that are appropriate to each context. We cannot know things (including Transcendent reality, however expressed) directly, but only as we perceive them or apprehend their impact. This is an alluring but excessively rational reductionism: mystics in the various faiths may have a different tale to tell – emphasizing a direct union with ultimate reality. It is also a very Western way of thinking, with its emphasis upon a sharp distinction between subject and object, leading to what others see as an extreme and sometimes fanatical individualism.

Hick counters criticisms of his views by broadening his definition of salvation:

> Suppose, then, we define salvation in a very concrete way, as an actual change in human beings, a change which can be identified – when it *can* be identified – by its moral fruits. We then find that we are talking about something that is of central concern to each of the great world faiths. Each in its different way calls us to transcend the ego point of view, which is the source of all selfishness, greed, exploitation, cruelty and injustice, and to become re-centred in that ultimate mystery for which we, in our Christian language, use the term God.

This definition may, ironically, be the sort of explanatory addition to his basic thesis that Hick condemns in others' beliefs. (He condemns those who add epicycles to their exclusivist, Ptolemaic worldview.) Moreover, his Western, Kantian, subject–object perspective does not easily coalesce with transcending the ego. Further, this definition of salvation enables him to link it with liberation, so that he now prefers the hybrid term 'salvation/liberation'.[7] Yet the two concepts are rather different. Beverley Clack has persuasively argued that

> At this juncture ... a change from the language of salvation to the language of liberation is necessary. It seems to me that the challenge of feminist thinking lies in the way in which it has exposed the negative understanding of the natural world and the place of humanity within it assumed by much of the language of salvation. Moreover the language of salvation has been dependent upon the Genesis narrative of the Fall, a story which has been used against women who have been categorized by many of the leading theologians of the tradition as 'daughters of Eve', and thus responsible for the perilous state of fallen humanity.[8]

'Salvation', as many theologians describe it, is an overused and inexact term. It is often summarized along the following lines. God's grace is over all, and every human discerns it in some measure. But evil haunts human hearts and structures, so God elects a people, Israel, and then a person, Jesus, to overcome it. The triumph of Jesus over death provides the hope that God will raise humans to eternal life. He does so through a chosen people, the church, which is the sign and first fruit of God's purpose to save all. In the end, God will judge all humans, and the results of his verdict will bring surprises. It is therefore very important for everyone to consider his or her own position and response, rather than those of others.[9]

Aspects of this interpretation leave a bitter taste in the mouth. It often pretends a generosity that it does not actually extend to others. It may seem pious and affirming to leave the fate of others to God (what else, indeed, can a religious person do!), but people who make such statements do not usually recognize the validity of works of goodness and mercy done out of faith and belief. Imagine saying to a holy Hindu or Jew that, although they are observably good and decent people, Christians can make no deductions from that about their status before Transcendence. Such a point of view hardly coheres with the Jesus of the Gospels, who made much of the transformation in the life of people who seriously engaged with God's forgiving grace.[10] This summary is based upon only a particular interpretation of part of the biblical material. In English translations of the Hebrew Bible (the Christian Old Testament), 'salvation' is used to translate different Hebrew words. One of the basic Hebrew root words has among its meanings 'to be broad', 'to enlarge' or 'to grow spacious'. Therefore, 'deliverance', 'liberation' or some other word may often translate particular contexts better than 'salvation' or its cognate terms.

Moreover, an exclusivist position has not been the only tradition within the Christian churches. Justin Martyr (c. 100–165) first articulated the doctrine of the *logos spermatikos* (seed-bearing word), which allowed him to affirm that God had prepared the way for Jesus not just through the Hebrew Bible but also through Greek philosophy. His sentence 'Whatever has been well said belongs to us' was developed mainly within the Eastern church. This can sound like crass inclusivism, but it need not be such. It could intend, at least to some extent, a generous attitude towards the wider world of beliefs. Moreover, an element of inclusivism is a necessary part of every attitude towards the other; ironically, even pluralists are inclusivists at bottom, the more so for not recognizing, as all must do, that all people view things from their own perspective.

The ancient churches of the East may have much to teach Christians about living faithfully in a world of religious diversity. This is partly because they have long co-existed with other groups, as minorities within predominantly Islamic or Hindu contexts. Moreover, from early times the Eastern church's intellectuals took the thoughts of Justin and other fathers like him more seriously than did those of the Western church. Paulos Mar Gregorios, formerly Metropolitan of Delhi and the North in the Malankara Orthodox Church, has written that

> If there is one thing we can surely say about India's cultural heritage, it is that that heritage has never been uniform or non-religious. I grew up as a Christian in the midst of that heritage; I went to a school where about a third were Christians, the others following Islam or different varieties of Sanatana Dharma [Hinduism based on the ancient Vedic scriptures]. As a child, I was not brainwashed by Western missionary thinking forcing me to regard and condemn non-Christians as unsaved ... [In later years] I saw the damage done to the image and reality of the Christian Church by the unchristian attitude towards other religions fostered by reformed thinkers such as Barth, Brunner and Kraemer. They were speaking out of their cultural parochialism rather than from any genuine Christian insight, it seemed to me.[11]

To some extent this is an optimistic view. To use Christian terminology, the Orthodox churches are no freer from sin than are any other Christian organizations, as is illustrated by the widespread anti-Semitism of the Russian Orthodox Church, and the prevalent Islamophobia of the Serbian Orthodox Church. Nevertheless, wherever the Orthodox churches have communicated the Christian message, many of their thinkers and practitioners have tried to take seriously the religious and wider cultural contexts of their converts as worthy of respect. Many of the original inhabitants (often designated 'the first people') of Alaska and Shintoists in Japan, who were converted by Orthodox Christians, were encouraged by them to esteem their roots and not to be ashamed or contemptuous of them.[12] This contrasts with the arrogant racism of many Western Christian missionaries, though of course there were many Western Christian missionaries who were wonderful witnesses of God's love for all people, religions and cultures.[13]

The prevailing view of religious pluralism – which employs the three categories of exclusivism, inclusivism and pluralism – operates within a Christian frame of reference. A few liberal and scholarly members of other religions have adopted this discourse, usually to commend the pluralist position,[14] but many more have not. To them, salvation, defined as a category that denotes a person's ultimate destination in heaven or hell, looks like a very Christian concern or even obsession.

For all the criticisms that can and should be levelled at this prevailing model, it has been a serious attempt to move forward to a more open and accepting attitude towards other faiths.

There have been other attempts, less dominated by Christian scholars and Western philosophical categories, to denote the acceptability of at least aspects of all religions. A particularly influential attempt is the *philosophia perennis*, or perennial philosophy. This was popularized in English by a book by Aldous Huxley.[15] In earlier years of the twentieth century, this view was associated with the Hindu scholar Ananda Coomaraswamy, the Muslim savant Frithjof Schuon and even the great Roman Catholic scholar of Islam, Louis Massignon. More recently, the Muslim Seyyed Hossein Nasr and the Christian Huston Smith have held it with particular clarity. Huxley described this philosophy as

> The metaphysic that recognizes a divine Reality substantial to the world of things and lives and minds; the psychology that finds in the soul something similar to, or even identical with, divine Reality; the ethic that places man's final end in the knowledge of the immanent and transcendent Ground of all being – the thing is immemorial and universal.[16]

The perennial philosophy teaches that outward aspects of the world's religions are diverse and often even contradictory. However, the inward aspects point to a single absolute. In the cosmos, the one (Absolute) becomes many (phenomena) through a series of hierarchical levels, through which the individual can ascend to the truth. The path on which individuals travel necessitates them embracing the outward form as well as the inward meaning of the religious tradition they espouse. Advocates believe that the perennial philosophy is very old, found in humankind's earliest primal experiences of faith, as well as in the great religions of the modern world.

The perennial philosophy is a seductive interpretation of the world's religions. It offers, in a rapidly secularizing world, a sense of the sacred that lives within all the religious traditions, a wisdom to which all humans therefore have access. Further, it allows for, indeed insists upon, individuals committing themselves to a religious path, rather than picking and choosing bits from each faith as is done by some advocates of the New Age or post-modernism. The sacred wisdom of the perennial philosophers may be compared to a fountainhead gushing forth water at the top of a hill. The streams flow their independent courses down the hill. They do not meet and mingle on their routes, but rather their underlying unity is in the source. So there may be many outward differences and contradictions between the faiths, many fundamental divergences of beliefs; yet there is a fundamental absolute from which they draw their resources to inspire and make wise *homo religiosus*, the religious human.

The problem with the perennial philosophy is that it is, at bottom, dependent on (admittedly very eloquent and learned) assertion, and is not susceptible to rational argument. Moreover, although it permits, even demands, a recognition that God encounters humans through many ways of faith and religion, proponents still have their axes to grind. For example, Nasr is sternly condemnatory of much phenomenal Christianity while having an idealized view of his own religion, Islam. Furthermore, there is a kind of Platonic elitism about the *philosophia perennis*. Many of its authors give the impression of being superior people who have discerned a wisdom open to all but really embraced by only a few astute and exceptional people.[17]

RETURNING TO ROOTS

Many creative scholars who write about issues of religious pluralism seem to sit light on their religious origins. Proponents of an ideological pluralism and adherents of the *philosophia perennis* are often at the edge of their religion or even outside the camp. Is this a necessary place to be?

A recent book edited by Heim, *Grounds for Understanding* (subtitled 'Ecumenical Resources for Responses to Religious Pluralism'), explores the ability and means of several Christian denominations to live appropriately in a religiously diverse world. Some of the articles are better than others, and none of them is really distinguished, but the idea behind the book is surely an excellent one. So much is heard today of the world's religions as malevolent institutions, violent and antagonistic towards others. It seems a good proposal to stress that there are other internal resources for peace and goodwill. This book does so by exploring varieties of resources by which Christians can engage creatively with others. It would be helpful if other religions produced similar works, admitting there can be a variety of responses towards others, and choosing those that are appropriate in today's world.

Such academic explorations underline the need for exponents of dialogue to be rooted within their traditions, where they can find resources for their openness towards others. Since I am myself a Methodist, I shall explore the roots of my tradition to explain how I can justify believing about and acting towards others in the ways that I do. It has been observed that Methodist Christians have been influential in the contemporary inter-religious dialogue out of all proportion to their actual numbers in the diverse world of Christianity. In an amusing and insightful article, Rebekah Miles has asked, 'John Wesley as Inter-religious Resource: Would You Take This Man to an Interfaith Dialogue?'[18] She demonstrates that Wesley (1703–1791), the founder of the Methodist movement, was quite capable, like many an English eighteenth-century polemicist, of damning Muslims and others in intemperate language. Nevertheless, she notes that he never says that non-Christians are damned; even at his most pessimistic, Wesley believed that knowledge of God's existence could be deduced from creation, and he came to believe that non-Christians could come to know much about God without the aid of Christian resources.

Miles's interesting and novel point is that Wesley's affirmation or condemnation of other faiths was grounded in his pastoral desire to encourage his Christian communities to live holy lives. So a positive appreciation of members of other faiths was intended to shame Methodists into improving their own lives. His sometimes negative assessment of others can be explained as a means to encourage Methodists to contrast the holiness to which they were called with the beastliness of others. This attitude can be attributed to the context in which he lived, rife as it was with anti-Semitism and Islamophobia: Jews had been officially allowed back in England only since 1656, after their expulsion in 1290; and Muslim Turks had besieged the gates of Vienna in 1683, thereby confirming Western European paranoia about Islam as a religion of the sword that intended to surround conquer and convert Christian Europe.

We shall look at Wesley's attitude towards Jews and Muslims to assess the truth of Miles's argument. Afterwards, we shall underline the importance of the New Testament story of Cornelius in Wesley's teaching. Then we shall indicate the attitude of modern interfaith Methodists towards their faith, to see how they rate their faith's importance for the dialogical life they live.

John Wesley met Jews in Savannah while he was a missionary in Georgia, USA, in 1737. On 4 April 1737, the day after Palm Sunday, Wesley recorded, 'I began learning Spanish, in order to converse with my Jewish parishioners; some of whom seem nearer the mind that was in Christ than many of those who call him Lord.'[19] Holy Week has never been high on the Jewish list of good times to be in the mind of Christians, some of whom have taken the opportunity at that time to kill those regarded as Christ killers. Even so, despite the passage's condescension (Jews as his parishioners, indeed!), and despite the fact that he uses actions of Jews as a stick with which to beat substandard Christians (a common Christian ploy, used by Martin Luther and many others; which seems to corroborate Miles's point that Wesley praised members of other faiths to encourage or even shame Methodists into being better), it is significant that Wesley recognized spiritual goodness, or holiness, when he saw it. There is also a little evidence that while in Georgia he absent-mindedly engaged in Christian–Jewish dialogue with his Spanish teacher. His journal for 7 July 1737 records that

> I was unawares engaged in a dispute with Dr. Nunes, a Jew, concerning the Messiah. For this afterwards I was much grieved, lest the truth might suffer by my weak defence of it.[20]

This is a tantalizing entry. Nunes was a Spanish Jew, engaged by Wesley to teach him Spanish. But we know nothing else about this dialogue.

Wesley sometimes had less positive reactions to Jews. In his journal, only a year later but after his return from Georgia and a few short months after his conversion, he described a visit to the famous Jewish synagogue in Rotterdam on 8 September:

> Having waited till past four in the afternoon, we stepped into the Jews' Synagogue, which lies near the water-side. I do not wonder that so many Jews (especially those who have any reflection) utterly abjure all religion. My spirit was moved within me at that horrid, senseless pageantry, that mockery of God, which they called public worship. Lord, do not thou yet 'cast off thy people!' But in Abraham's 'Seed' let them also 'be blessed!'

This passage shows how much Wesley shared the anti-Semitic prejudices of many of his contemporaries. It may also show his English reserve and priggishness. Earlier that day, in his own words,

> we went to the English Episcopal Church [in Rotterdam], which is a large, handsome, convenient building. The minister read prayers seriously and distinctly to a small, well-behaved congregation.

Maybe Dutch Jews enjoyed themselves more than the English abroad. After Wesley's visit to the synagogue, he recorded that 'The ship lingering still, I had time to exhort several English whom we met to pursue inward religion, the renewal of their souls in righteousness and true holiness.'[21] Very edifying: the themes of righteousness and holiness are central to Wesley's religion. Yet there remains a lingering suspicion that he was unable to see that righteousness and holiness can be pursued in different ways than his own; they cannot be labelled as untrue simply because he has no empathy for nor real understanding of alternative expressions of them.

One more reference from many years later, almost but not quite an appreciative one, is recorded in his journal for 23 February 1770:

> I was desired to hear Mr. Leoni sing at the Jewish synagogue [at Duke's Place, Aldgate; he was a chorister there, and his proper name was Meyer Lyon]. I never before saw a Jewish congregation behave so decently. Indeed, the place is itself so solemn that it might strike an awe upon those who have any thought of God.[22]

Despite the condescension, it is clear that Wesley was truly moved by what he saw. My own impression of reading Wesley's words about Jews is that Miles is right that Wesley was primarily interested in the pastoral task of encouraging and uplifting his Christian congregations. Still, other things were also at issue. There is a genuine if guarded sense of appreciation that emerges from some of his few references to Jews.

What about Wesley and the world of Islam? Notoriously, in 1783, he wrote of Muslims that they are 'as utter strangers to all true religion as their four-footed brethren; as void of mercy as lions and tigers; as much given up to brutal lusts as bulls or goats. So that they are in truth a disgrace to human nature.'[23] Yet, late in life, when he was eighty-four years old, he preached a sermon entitled 'On Faith'. This particular sermon raises the issue of faith in relation to the world's religions. His text was from the New Testament book of Hebrews, chapter 11, verse 6: 'Without faith it is impossible to please God.' He did not use this text to dismiss other interpretations of religion than his own. Rather, he wrote of degrees of faith: from the lowest form, that of the 'materialist' (by which he meant someone who 'believes that there is nothing but matter in the universe') to the highest, that of Protestant Christians, which 'embraces only those truths as necessary to salvation which are clearly revealed in the oracles of God'.[24] This sermon attracts the editorial comment that 'it comes closer to an explicit statement of his vision of universal saving grace than anything else in the Wesley canon'.[25] In it, Wesley leads his hearers and readers onwards and upwards, through the faith of a materialist, a deist, a heathen (to which he joins the faith of a 'Mahometan', by which he means Muslim), a

Jew, the special faith of John the Baptist, then Roman Catholic and finally Protestant Christians.

This hierarchical model that leads inexorably to the validation of Wesley's own position may register unfavourably with modern readers. Yet in his day and age, his was a remarkably open and generous viewpoint. His broad-minded approach included Islam. Although he dismisses many heathen as savages, he comments,

> But many of them, especially in the civilized nations, we have great reason to hope, although they lived among heathens, yet were quite of another spirit; being taught of God, by his inward voice, all the essentials of true religion. Yea, and so was that Mahometan, an Arabian, who a century ago wrote the life of Hai Ebn Yokdan. The story seems to be feigned; but it contains all the principles of pure religion and undefiled.[26]

The story (which Wesley was correct in believing feigned) actually originated among medieval Islamic philosophers, a number of whom recounted it. (It became the basis of *Robinson Crusoe* by Daniel Defoe, who was a contemporary of Wesley). The most famous teller of this tale was the Spanish Muslim Ibn Tufayl (who died in 1185 or 1186). Hai Ebn Yokdan comes from an Arabic name, meaning 'The Living One, Son of the Wake'. Ibn Tufayl's Hayy Ibn Yaqzan (a better transliteration of the names than Wesley's) was a man who, left on an island as a baby, grew up without human company and was reared by animals. During his long life he discovered many laws of nature by sheer observation and by dint of his natural intelligence. As he observed animal life, he learned the rules of society and the reason for societal rules. He became a deeply ethical being. Late in life, he managed to get over to another island with a large human population. Society there lived by a code of ethics taught by a prophet who had received it in the form of revelations from God. Hayy Ibn Yaqzan was awestruck to discover that those revelations agreed exactly with the conclusions he had arrived at during his contemplations in complete solitude on his desert island.

Wesley was not aware of this intra-Islamic debate between medieval philosophers and theologians about how one could know about the good life: did God have to reveal it, as the theologians believed; or were the truths God revealed through the prophets accessible to unaided human reason, as philosophers tended to think? The important point is that the evidence forced Wesley to admit that goodness and grace ('holiness' was his preferred term) were available to all humans, because God is the God of all people, not some localized deity who is indifferent or even bad-tempered towards the vast majority of humans who are not members of his particular club. In Wesley's case, the evidence was based on scanty experience, and more upon the evaluation of written sources. In this sermon, he admitted that

> With heathens, Mahometans, and Jews, we have at present nothing to do; only we may wish that their lives did not shame many of us that are called Christians. We have not much more to do with the members of the Church of Rome[27]

This quotation rather supports Miles's view that Wesley used such knowledge as he had of other religions for the pastoral upbraiding of his Methodist people. But that was not the only strand. I would argue that his inclusive theology, which emphasized God's love for all rather than a few people, was based on his reading of scripture and was not simply a useful ploy to lick his followers into shape. In particular, Wesley was shaped by, even obsessed with, the story of Cornelius. Cornelius was a centurion in the Roman army of occupation, who, after receiving an angelic visitation, sent for the apostle Peter and was baptized with his entire household. This story is told in the book of Acts, chapters 10 and 11. On 2 August 1745, Wesley wrote a series of questions for his preachers, to which, with characteristic thoroughness and confidence, he supplied the answers. For questions 7 to 9 he wrote:

> Q.7 Have we duly considered the case of Cornelius? Was not he in the favour of God, when 'his prayers and alms came up for a memorial before God'; that is, before he believed in Christ?

> A. It does seem that he was, in some degree. But we speak not of those who have not heard the gospel.

> Q.8 But were these works of his 'splendid sins'?[28]

> A. No; nor were they done without the grace of Christ.

> Q.9 How then can we maintain, that all works done before we have a sense of the pardoning love of God are sin, and, as such, an abomination to Him?

> A. The works of him who has heard the gospel, and does not believe, are not done as God hath 'willed and commanded them to be done.' And yet we know not how to say that they are an abomination to the Lord in him that feareth God, and, from that principle, does the best he can.[29]

In his commentary on the story of Cornelius in *Explanatory Notes on the New Testament* (1754), Wesley had not changed his mind about the efficacy of pre-justification works but stressed also the incomparable value of explicit faith in God through Christ. In his notes on Acts 10:35, he wrote,

> **But in every nation he that feareth him, and worketh righteousness** – He that first reverences God, as great, wise, good; the Cause, End, and Governor of all things; and, secondly, from this awful regard to Him, not only avoids all known evil, but endeavours, according to the best light he has, to do all things well. **Is accepted of him** – Through Christ, though he knows Him not. The assertion is express, and admits of no exception. He is in the favour of God, whether enjoying His written word and ordinances or not. Nevertheless, the addition of these is an unspeakable blessing to those who were before, in some measure, accepted: otherwise, God would never have sent an angel from heaven to direct Cornelius to St. Peter.[30]

Wesley's agonizing over the place of Jesus in God's universal grace was hardly related to the world of religions, but to his mission among the 'unchurched' in Britain and Ireland and to his defence of inclusive Arminian over exclusive Calvinist interpretations of Christian belief. Despite occasional references to other faiths by the Wesley brothers, there is truth in John Munsey Turner's observation that 'the impact of the reality of God in other religions ... was just over [John] Wesley's horizon'.[31]

Wesley's commitment to Jesus as revealing the universal love of God has had a profound impact among many Methodists. But modern Methodists live in a very different world. So how can Methodists today draw inspiration from Wesley's words? One could follow Rebekah Miles's insight and argue that, despite Wesley's strictures about world religions other than Christianity, his practical or pastoral theology permits us to be godly and goodly towards those who believe differently from us. But that is to play down, as so many British historians and some North American theologians have done, the theological insightfulness, if not perfect systematic coherence, of his writings. He knew, on the basis of Christian faith, that all humans can grow into goodness and grow into God, as his allusions to the stories of Cornelius and of Hayy Ibn Yaqzan indicate. To put it in personal terms, Wesley's doctrine of holiness has encouraged me to be the friend of all and the enemy of none, as far as in me lies the power to be so. I have discovered, as he did (though without the benefit I have had of living among diverse worlds of faith), that good works are often located in authentic human responses to the saving grace of Transcendent reality, however named or construed.

GROWING FROM ROOTS

The previous section argued that dialogical people should be rooted in their faith, interpreted in a tolerant and inclusive way. It would be possible to find other, more exclusive ways in the Methodist tradition of Christian faith. But in our diverse world, what would be the point of that?

So I prefer to delineate a Methodist tradition of hospitality and tolerance and openness towards others in the hope that it will encourage readers to explore their own religious resources for a generosity of spirit towards different interpretations of faith. Other Christian denominations and also Muslims, Buddhists, first peoples and many other religious people can discern within their traditions, however narrow some may wish to confine them, such liberality and charity towards others.

Many people in Wesley's day, as in ours, were bigoted in their attitude towards the wider world. But some were, to use his words, 'quite of another spirit'. Since Western Europeans, not least the English, have had a long colonial history of the exploitation and even destruction of people of other religions and cultures, it is salutary to rescue two more positive voices about saving faith as a universal human quality, open to all.

Shortly before Wesley's birth, King Charles II (who reigned from 1660 to 1685) granted American land to William Penn, the troublesome son of an admiral to whom the monarch owed sixteen thousand pounds. The tract of land became Pennsylvania. William Penn was an embarrassment to his father because he became a non-conformist, a Quaker, and squabbled endlessly with the establishment; and he was a remarkable man. He treated the North American native people as separate nations to respect and live alongside, rather than as threats or as primitive hindrances to civilized white people. This magnificent sentiment from 1693 illustrates his tolerance and broad-mindedness:

> The humble, meek, merciful, just, pious and devout souls are everywhere of one religion, and when death has taken off the mask, they will know one another, though the diverse liveries they wear here make them strangers.[32]

A younger contemporary of Wesley, William Blake (1757–1827), was a poet, painter, engraver and visionary. In *Songs of Innocence* (1789), published a year after Wesley's sermon 'On Faith', Blake wrote:

> To Mercy, Pity, Peace and Love,
> All pray in their distress;
> And to these virtues of delight
> Return their thankfulness.
>
> For Mercy, Pity, Peace and Love
> Is God, our father dear,
> And Mercy, Pity, Peace and Love
> Is Man, his child and care.
>
> For Mercy has a human heart,
> Pity a human face,
> And Love, the human form divine,
> Love, Mercy, Pity, Peace.
>
> Then every man, of every clime,
> That prays in his distress,
> Prays to the human form divine,
> Love, Mercy, Pity, Peace.
>
> And all must love the human form,
> In heathen, Turk or Jew;
> Where Mercy, Love and Pity dwell,
> There God is dwelling too.[33]

This remarkable poem speaks for itself. But it is worth pointing out that many Christian pluralists might find its inclusiveness discomfiting. Blake was no liberal-minded and uncommitted religious dilettante. The other songs in this poetical set are deeply Christological, mingling profound insights about humans and God from a Christian perspective.

Nowadays, it will not do simply to rely on Christian teaching; we need also to learn and listen from others. Yet Blake and Wesley both remind us that each of us does so from a particular context. The failure of much pluralist ideology is that it falls into Arnold Toynbee's grand error of assuming that the tree of knowledge has no roots from whence it grew. Christian pluralists play down Christology in favour either of concepts of Transcendent reality, however conceived, or of liberation/ salvation. Yet all of us come to our Transcendent knowledge by being rooted in a tradition, or from an experience or experiences of that over-arching reality, not by bypassing or playing down its central importance in shaping who we are. In the introduction to this book, I made this point by observing that it is better to be a flower than a butterfly. We are all rooted; beware of those dialogicians who do not understand this point and who therefore do not understand a central insight about religion as gift and givenness.

Dialogicians recognize that their own traditions' resources, interpreted in unprejudiced and open-minded ways, have shaped their attitude towards others, and this gives them the confidence to meet and listen to others in the hope and expectation that Transcendence has made her home among them. The convictions we have gained from our traditions can be tested for their truth by developing them in the light of what we see and hear of people of other faith.

Most humans are not yet able psychologically or doctrinally to be objective about faith statements. Indeed, faith does not yield its secrets in any form to those who aspire after bloodless objectivity – a slippery, rather lofty Toynbee-like aspiration. If it is desirable, in our global village, to work towards a common religious quest for truth, rather than simply seeking guidance from one's own particular perspective, then I would argue, as a Methodist, that as well as observing John Wesley's *explicit* encouragement to his followers to read and develop Christian faith in an open and inclusive fashion, we need also to follow his more *cautious*, often *implicit*, advice to recognize and affirm true holiness not just *wherever* but *however* it is found. When we do so, we shall usually discover that it is formed and sustained by Transcendent grace as people recognize and are seized by its alluring power. So my Jewish and Muslim friends are certainly attracted, empowered and sustained by God, whom Christians can recognize because of all he is and has done in Jesus of Nazareth. Yet Jews and Muslims would affirm that they are divinely loving and loved because of, in the one case, the gift of the Torah, and in the other, the revelation of the Sharia, the straight path of obedience to the divine law. A Buddhist friend would interpret faith and holiness differently again, as responding appropriately as one who has woken up from, or been liberated into, the world as it actually is rather than as it superficially appears to be.

I would suggest, as a deduction from John Wesley's position, that, given the world needs holiness, Methodists working by themselves or even in partnership with others cannot hope to transform situations. Religious people cannot mend the world by themselves. They need to do so working together for the common good.

Wesley was often very dismissive of 'opinions', by which he meant theological assertions that divide people rather than transform them. He accepted the classical doctrines of the church, as do his followers, but he saw them as a means to the end that people should be holy, not holier than thou.

So perhaps it is in the area of applied ethics rather than the purity of doctrine that Methodists can begin to influence and be influenced by people of other faith in the twenty-first century. Ibn Tufayl and other Muslim philosophers who recounted the story of Hayy Ibn Yaqzan wanted to convey the idea that ethics, to be true, must be universal; at least in the sense that people seeking the good life would have some coherent notion of, and strategies for, how to attain it in word and deed. Such intellectuals knew that Christians and Muslims (and Jews, too) are never going to agree on the precise form of pure and unalloyed monotheism. But an ethics devoid of theology would be a toothless lion, having little power over most people. In the process of ethical debate and endeavour, questions of truth will emerge in fresh and illuminating ways.

There are indications in most religions that the quality of people's faith is discerned in the lives that they lead. Jesus observed that not everyone who called him Lord would enter the kingdom of heaven, but those who do the will of his heavenly Father (Matthew 7:21). In Judaism, Jesus' own religion, the Noahide laws are the seven laws given to Noah, the father of humankind, after the flood. The doctrine dates from Rabbinic times, but is based on earlier biblical appeals to gentiles to behave with justice and equity. These laws imply that all humans know either instinctively, or by the religious tradition they follow, the basic laws that lead to the good life (we are close again to the thought behind the story of Hayy Ibn Yaqzan). Just as Jews must obey the Torah, so gentiles must follow the Noahide laws. Broadly speaking, these seven principles prohibit: idolatry, blasphemy, murder, adultery and incest (counted as one), and robbery. They command the need to establish a system of justice and prohibit the eating of flesh torn from a living animal. Gentiles are obliged to keep these laws. Each who does so is counted among 'the righteous of the nations of the world', who have a share in the life of the world to come.

In Islam, there are a number of attitudes towards members of other religions. Islamic scripture recognizes that different communities of faith will continue to exist even though Islam has been revealed, and offers an ethical test:

To each of you we have given a law and an open way. If God had had so willed, he would have made you a single people, but instead he tests you by what he has given you. So strive to excel in good deeds. Finally, you will all return to him, and he will show you the truth of the matters in which you were at variance. (Qur'an 5:48)

So, this growth from one's religious roots into appreciation of the faithful other could be justified from the teaching of many religions as primarily an ethical endeavour. However, this moral effort is not effected simply by human determination. False dichotomies are proposed in and between a number of religions about the superiority of either faith or works. In fact, most creeds contend that faith, interpreted as trust that this life (including one's own individual existence) is porous to Transcendent reality, can lead to holiness if one aligns oneself with its captivating and transforming power.

A GLOBAL ETHIC?

In recent years, there has been an attempt by many religious intellectuals to establish a universal ethic for the global village. This has happened at high levels. Early in 1989, the German theologian Hans Küng gave a paper to a colloquium at UNESCO in Paris. He repeated it the following month in Toronto and Chicago. Its English title was 'No Peace among the Nations without Peace among the Religions'. For Küng, this means there must be dialogue between the religions and an investigation of their foundations. From his enthusiasm blossomed a number of conferences, part of the momentum for a commitment to a global ethic that was accepted by the Parliament of the World's Religions at Chicago in 1993. Since then, a number of conferences have commented upon it, and organizations promoting a global ethic are mushrooming in the USA and Europe. Küng himself founded the Global Ethic Foundation at Tübingen in 1995, and this now has an ambitious educational programme.

There were significant stepping stones on the way to this global ethic. The General Assembly of the United Nations adopted the Universal Declaration of Human Rights on 10 December 1948. Since then, interfaith organizations like the World Conference on Religion and Peace and the International Association for Religious Freedom, as well as conferences organized by the Unification Church and the Brahma Kumaris, have made significant statements about the role of religions in establishing and sustaining peace. Since 1997, UNESCO has again become interested in clarifying and publicizing the aims and ideals of a global ethic.

The declaration on *The Principles of a Global Ethic* of the Parliament of the World's Religions has what it calls four irrevocable directives. They are: commitment to non-violence and respect for life; commitment to a culture of solidarity and a just economic order; commitment to a culture of tolerance and a life of truthfulness; and commitment to a culture of equal rights and partnership between men and women.[34] These are worthy aims, indeed.

However, one could offer three friendly criticisms of the declaration. First, although it strongly condemns some religious people for contributing to a lack of peace and justice in the world, it implies that they are unworthy representatives of their faiths. It does not recognize how easy it is even for peace-loving religious people to have blind spots. Second, despite the fact that the declaration recognizes that there are too many old answers to new challenges in the modern world, it does not always appreciate the fact, still less the importance, of innovative trends in religions today. Third, some distinguished advocates of the global ethic tend, surprisingly, to oversimplify the issues at stake.

One blind spot can be illustrated by examining part of the last of the directives: commitment to a culture of partnership between men and women. This points to the resources of religions to bring about such a desirable goal. It does not explicitly admit the involvement of religions in justifying the subordination and oppression of women by men. One aspect of this is the invisibility of women. Of course, religions are not alone in overlooking women. The contribution of women has been hauntingly absent from other areas of human life. Over fifty years ago, Simone de Beauvoir, in her book *The Second Sex* (1949), pointed out that from Socrates to Sartre, her companion, few women had been philosophers, and philosophers had not addressed the role of women in fresh and positive ways.

Yet religions need to look inwards at this issue, hopefully to heal rather than to justify.[35] Even at the source of religions, the sacred texts or foundational figures held in great reverence by devotees sometimes ignore women. This area requires enormous sensitivity, that extraordinarily difficult and delicate task of negotiating and translating between different cultures and worlds, so as to be faithful to the tradition and faithful to what it means to be transformed humans here and now.

There *are* remarkable examples of the transformative contribution of men and women working together in contemporary religious life. For example, when I attended Friday midday prayers at Claremont Main

Road Mosque in Cape Town on 30 August 1996, the preacher was the Dean Designate of the city's Anglican cathedral. Men and women sat alongside each other in the mosque. There was a genuine attempt to involve men and women in partnership.

In his acclaimed book *An Intimate History of Humanity* Theodore Zeldin writes, 'I have chosen to write about women, because I am not one myself, and because I have always preferred to write about subjects which do not tempt me to be so arrogant as to believe that I can ever understand them, but above all because many women seem to me to be looking at life with fresh eyes.'[36] Zeldin's book compels us to look at the world afresh in order to be transformed. Many proponents of a global ethic do not look at religions with enough wide-eyed wonder.

A second friendly criticism of the 1993 directive is that it does not show sufficient recognition of and openness to innovation and diversity in the contemporary religious scene. For example, let us look at part of the third irrevocable directive of the global ethic: commitment to a culture of tolerance. The expansion of this principle in the text emphasizes honesty and truthfulness. Let us pause on this matter of tolerance. In English, is 'tolerance' such a promising word? When we say, 'I tolerate you', well, it is better than the alternative, 'I do not tolerate you', but not exactly a full vote of confidence and equality. Even so, how difficult it is for religions to deal with tolerance; more difficult than the directive countenances, particularly in the matter of freedom to choose one's religion. The *Shorter Oxford English Dictionary* defines 'tolerance' as 'the disposition to be patient with the opinions or practices of others; forbearance; catholicity of spirit'. This sounds good, but can it survive or is it even adequate as an ideal when religions challenge each other in matters of fundamental belief and practice?

Stephen Banfield's biography of the twentieth-century composer Gerald Finzi raises this matter in an interesting way. Finzi was completely Jewish: Sephardi on his paternal side; Ashkenazi on his maternal. The book's subtitle is, perceptively, 'An English Composer'. Finzi was born in London and reared in Harrogate. He lived through the Holocaust and helped to rescue some Jews from Hitler's Germany. Even so, many of his closest friends did not know he was Jewish. In adulthood he embraced a rural English existence as to the manner born, growing apples in Hampshire and painstakingly working on relatively few musical works. Finzi's masterpiece is *Dies Natalis*, a setting from the seventeenth-century English mystic Thomas Traherne's *Centuries of*

Meditation. The text is quintessentially English, as is its musical setting. I, who love wandering amid religious and cultural diversity, feel, when I hear Finzi's setting of Traherne's words, that I have come home. The slow movements of his clarinet and cello concertos also evoke an Englishness that can no doubt be explained in terms of musical form and structure but is not exhausted or even much illuminated by *that* particular explanation. Finzi hid his Jewishness and affected an Englishness that some could see as a parody; yet I find it utterly moving.

However, in an appalling century for Jews, to abandon Jewishness, for whatever reasons, can seem like granting Hitler a posthumous victory – to allude to Emil Fackenheim's phrase.[37] In particular, marrying outside the community, as Finzi did, has caused a collapse in Jewish numbers in Britain and the USA and has made many Jews raise again that poignant question: who is a Jew? Other small communities face this problem, for example the Parsees in India. It is not just inter-marriage or conversion to another religion or to secularism that proves problematic. Many old religious questions are being asked in new, exciting and even unnerving ways, and many new questions are being asked. The work of scholars like John Berthrong on 'multiple religious participation',[38] belonging to more than one religion, can seem threatening or even destructive to many religious people, not least to those from numerically small groups. (We shall explore this phenomenon more thoroughly in Chapter 5.) Yet this fusion of faiths remains an increasing possibility in the religious world of the new century, as people meet, mix, meditate and maybe even marry or at least mate. Arguably, multiple religious participation has been practised in East Asia for centuries. How can others tolerate it yet find a place for religious groupings that are utterly threatened by it? It is not surprising that there are many internal debates in Judaism and the Parsee religion about whether traditional notions of membership can be extended. Here are old questions in new guises, more agonizing to deal with than the global ethic recognizes.

A third criticism of the 1993 directive concerns a certain innocence of the issues involved in bringing this splendid project to locate a global ethic to a successful conclusion. For example, some of its proponents assume too easily that religions ought to accept the authority of, or at least work with, secular international organizations. Former President Ali Khamenei of Iran stated, 'When we want to find out what is right and wrong, we do not go to the United Nations; we go to the Holy Koran.' He went on to say, more colourfully, 'For us the Universal Declaration of Human Rights is nothing but a collection of mumbo-jumbo by disciples of Satan.'[39] His is far from the only view in contemporary Islam towards ethics, peace and human rights. Yet proponents of a global ethic need to understand and deal with the impulses that lead many religious people to say and believe such things; or else they will condemn their important project to sentimental, platitudinous irrelevance.

Distinguished enthusiasts like Hans Küng and Leonard Swidler have located the Golden Rule in many religions, and proffer it as a cure for the world's ills. This is the teaching that we should treat others as we ourselves would wish to be treated. So the Native American Great Law of Peace runs, 'The foundation is respect for all life'; and the *Analects* of Confucius (15:23) asserts, 'Do not do unto others what you would not have them do unto you.' This can be paralleled in most or maybe all religious traditions.[40]

There are a number of reservations to be made. One important one is the tendency among the proponents of the Golden Rule to offer easy, oversimplistic ways through complex ethical, political and social relations between religious people. The first-century BCE Rabbi Hillel must have been a wonderfully quirky man. Some people tried to irritate him by asking him silly questions.

One said, 'Why do Babylonians have round heads?'

'My son, you have asked a great question,' Hillel replied. 'Because they have no skilful midwives.'

He used humour as part of his teaching method to defuse animosity and to get others to think and move beyond their trite assumptions. One might light-heartedly contend that he was Jewish, after all, and Jews are famous for their wit. When a heathen came to him to ask him to teach him the whole Torah standing on one leg, Hillel replied, 'That which is hateful to you do not do to your neighbour. This is the whole of the Torah. The rest is commentary.' Serious-minded proponents of a global ethic have pounced on this as the Jewish illustration of a universal impulse towards a Golden Rule. Yet Hillel probably accepted the essentially trivial approach of this seeker after truth in palatable form, in order, by wit and wisdom, to lead him deeper into the ocean of truth.[41] A further problem about the establishment of a global ethic could be that it might become the ethical equivalent of the pluralist theological agenda, constructing an agenda out there that is not only generalized and naïve but also fails to take seriously one's roots.

So, if we seek peace in the world, we must not be sentimental and simplistic about core values, or locate agreement and even difference between religions in the wrong places. We need not only an ethic of agreement but also an ethic for coping with disagreement, where religions have wronged others. For example, Dalits in India, the oppressed or burdened ones, marginalized and even dehumanized by many other Indians, have little reason to value or trust the teachings of the Sanskritic traditions of Hinduism, which they see as the ideological justification for their subjugation. Any ethic we pursue has to recognize the need for justice and the integrity of creation, and avoid any spurious harmonization that papers over profound inequities.

The global ethic is a brave and admirable attempt to harness the resources of the world's religions to positive and universal ends. Yet religions cannot just be applied like balm for the soul in order to produce desirable ends like peace and justice. They must not simply admire their theoretical resources. They have to reform themselves in the contemporary world if they are truly to be homes for the human spirit. They must learn from each other and explore each other's deepest resources for faithful adaptation to the context of our global village. For this reason, I reckon the study of religious spiritualities appropriate for the new millennium to be among the more pressing tasks of the religions and the academy. I think the ancient wisdom to which the declaration refers is to be found in matters of religious spirituality more than in the Golden Rule.

Hans Küng and others have given us an interesting model to begin our work to establish peace among the religions, spreading outwards from them into other areas of human life. We shall need to refine and extend that model for the third millennium if we are to answer the question: is there a common ethic underlying all religious endeavour and experience? This question has become increasingly urgent in a world under the threat of nuclear annihilation. If humans could point to a common thread of teaching that seems to describe how Transcendence lures humans towards the good, then we might be able to promote the things that make for peace. But this needs to be grounded in the complex realities of life, not in sentimental or unfocused generalities. Any ethic we pursue that would ensure the world's survival has to recognize the need for justice towards other humans and also the integrity of creation, and to avoid any spurious harmonization that papers over profound inequities.

There is one other consideration. The search for a global ethic may have fooled us into believing that it is possible and desirable to take the other's deeds more seriously than their beliefs. Although it can seem more sensible for people of different religions to agree on practices that both feel able to pursue, rather than on beliefs that divide them, this is an alluring mistake. Many religious people do what they do because of what they believe. Wesley's concept of holiness or perfect love, the Jewish Noahide laws, and the Qur'an's insistence that communities should strive to do good deeds, although luminously ethical in their emphases, depend on a theological stance about what sort of God that God is. Good theology often leads to good deeds, but bad theology often leads to bad ones. So I would argue that, in a religiously diverse world, we need to embark on the enterprise of exploring an inter-religious theology of religions. To this issue, we now turn.

3 DIALOGUE IN THE NEW MILLENNIUM

RELIGION IN THE CONTEMPORARY WORLD

Since the end of the Second World War the religious map of the world has changed extraordinarily, most likely more than in any other period of history. The heartland of Christianity has moved south. The Christian faith has grown in the churches of Africa and even in parts of Asia, a continent that has been notably resistant to Christian missionary activity: South Korea is one Asian country where Christianity is growing apace. Large parts of the Islamic world have been freed from the yoke of Western political imperialism. This has led, among other things, to renewed internal debate among many Muslim men and women about the meaning of Islamic law, to take account of, for example, social justice perspectives and what constitutes the notion of the ideal society. Yet some Islamic countries have reacted to this domestic discussion with rejection and even violence, within and without the House of Islam. Inclusive and tolerant views in Hinduism, which have dominated that family of religions since the nineteenth century, found expression in the early years of independent India, which was declared a secular state. These broad-minded views were associated with such giant figures as Swami Vivekananda, who made an enormous impression at the first World Parliament of Religions, held in Chicago in 1893; and Mahatma Gandhi, who was murdered by a Hindu 'fundamentalist' in January 1948. Recent trends have led to the revival of a much more self-conscious association of Hinduism with the essential significance of India itself, and a more critical interpretation of, and even violent reaction towards, other religions that flourish there, especially Islam. The Tibetan form of Buddhism was transformed after the Chinese occupation of Tibet in 1950. It may seem that there is little future for Tibetan Buddhism in its homeland, but it has proved to be a compelling philosophy to many people in parts of North India, California and other far-flung places where *émigré* monks have settled. The creation of the state of Israel in 1948 provided Jews with a hope of safe space after the horror of six million Jews murdered in Nazi death camps. Yad Vashem, the Holocaust memorial site near Jerusalem, provides the visitor with an interpretation of Israel as the answer to the Holocaust, and plays down the continuing importance of the Jewish diaspora. These are just a few brief examples from some major world faiths.

Alongside transformations of the major world religions has been the renewal of primal faith. Many North Americans have rediscovered their links with religious traditions that pre-date the coming of Europeans. In Africa, Asia and Australasia, the indigenous religions have undergone a renaissance or else have greatly affected the religions that many thought would replace and obliterate them. The distinguished Africanist Geoffrey Parrinder, writing in the late 1940s and early 1950s about African traditional religion in a part of western Nigeria, believed such religion to be on its way out and wrote two chapters of Wagnerian solemnity about this, called 'The Twilight of the Gods'.[1] From our vantage point in time, his judgement looks uncharacteristically wide of the mark.

Then there is the proliferation of new religious movements (often shortened to NRMs). One example is the Unification Church, founded as the Holy Spirit Association for the Unification of World Christianity by the Reverend Sun Myung Moon in Korea in 1954. The Reverend Moon, as his followers (often called 'Moonies') refer to him, declared himself to be the Messiah at a banquet in Seoul in July 1992. To be precise, he said, in Korean, that 'My wife ... and I are the True Parents of all humanity ... We are the saviour, the Lord of the Second Advent, the Messiah.'[2] (I was present on that occasion; a fascinating experience for a student of religious studies. Many of the Jews and Christians present had an amicable conversation with each other about whether he could theoretically be a or the Messiah, though none thought that he actually was that figure. The Muslims, however, were uniformly hostile to the claim.) The Unification Church is quite small in numbers, with only about ten thousand followers in the West. Still, NRMs are often disproportionately influential with respect to the size of their membership;

they tend to attract educated articulate, middle-class, well-educated young people. There are many NRMs in the world today, often mushrooming out of the major world religions. Although Hindus often accept Hindu-based NRMs as a legitimate modern expression of ancient faith, most other religions regard them as eccentric at best, demonic at worst.

These are only a few examples of the significant changes in the pattern of religions around the world since the middle years of the twentieth century. A number of recent books have begun to posit the notion that a global consciousness has developed during that period, and to assess the changing map of religion as a factor in that new historical development, and its role in strengthening and interpreting that development.[3]

A GLOBAL CONSCIOUSNESS: FACT OR FICTION? VISION OR NIGHTMARE?

Is it really credible to look forward to, or even inwards at, a world more bound together than ever before as a real fact and a positive achievement? The contemporary world has certainly been inter-linked by unprecedented scientific and technological advances. When I flew to Singapore in 1956, it took days to get there and the plane refuelled in exotic places like Brindisi, Karachi and Calcutta. Now it is a thirteen-hour non-stop flight. When I typed my M.Phil. thesis in 1982, I had to redo innumerable pages where my fingers slipped or when my brain wandered from a coherent train of thought. Now, spell-check, cut-and-paste, drag-and-drop and a host of other alluring computer tools can help rescue academics from our natural incompetence; and, when we get bored, we can check our email or surf the web for a few moments until we gain renewed interest in the real task in hand.

What is less easy to do than to illustrate the recent networking of the world is to assess its significance. There are reasons to welcome, at least theoretically, the unifying of the world by science, technology and economics. But the twentieth century was a century of genocide: two world wars, the Armenian massacres, Stalin's purges of his opponents in the USSR in the 1930s, the Holocaust, and the killing fields of Cambodia and Rwanda are but some examples. We could also cite the destruction of many smaller cultures and languages, and the massive disappearance of various non-human life forms. So it is not surprising that visionary men and women look to a future in which people are close bound by things that make for justice and peace.

Even so, some have questioned glib assumptions about the fact of globalization, let alone its positive significance. What about the poor and dispossessed of the world, who have little knowledge of the world outside their own lives, which are boundaried by hunger and lack of opportunity? Critics of theories of globalization have pointed out that rich people in Chicago, Cambridge and Calcutta have more in common with each other than with the destitute outside their fine houses and offices.[4] Still, the fact that small elites in such places speak English in the public arena, communicate with each other by fax and email, wear suits to work and eat Thai food or the latest faddy victuals chosen from the smorgasbord of the world's cuisine does not disprove globalization; quite the opposite, in fact. What this fact does do is ask about the morality of it. Coca Cola and McDonald's burgers have become symbols of products, available almost everywhere on the planet, that profit the few rather than the many. Such merchandise is not absolutely essential for survival, whatever many young children might think. For religious people, this state of affairs begs searching questions about what faith can offer to overcome the social and economic exploitation of certain aspects of globalization. Can religion help the real fact of globalization to become a positive achievement for the human race in the twenty-first century?

Some scholars think not; not just those who are religiously tone deaf, but also others who are devout yet gloomy or perhaps clear sighted about the shortcomings of religion as a human phenomenon. Although some books in the field of religious studies confidently lay before their readers a vision of a growing global spirituality that will regenerate the religious consciousness of humankind and rescue it from its worst excesses, others are pessimistic about the future of religions in a global era, believing them to lag behind other fields of academic endeavour. To be sure, some scholars of religion in a plural society, even distinguished ones, have a tendency to treat religion in an idealistic, uncontextual way. Much work by religious scholars about the need to establish a global ethic and what it would look like illustrates this rather shallow and sentimental tendency; but not all such work.[5]

In fact, religious commitment remains important to most people. However, religions themselves are less enduring phenomena than is religion. Human history is littered with the wreckage of dead religions, many of whose adherents must have thought they would last eternally. Presumably, some of those devotees were just as sure that their beliefs were the last word as are today's religious fundamentalists. Within the enormous changes in the religious map of the world of the last half-century, one can perhaps detect signs of decline in some expressions of some religions. In Western Europe, institutional Christianity is in deep decline and often seems to be in the hands of those who aim to hasten its demise. Like African primal faith, Western Christianity may yet make a comeback, even if in forms that we would not easily recognize. More-over, in most parts of the world, institutional religion continues to be an important phenomenon, helping adherents to construct social realities. Recent surveys in the USA suggest that fifty-two per cent of the population attends a place of worship on a regular basis.

Since religion has endured from the earliest times as a persistent expression of humankind's openness to the conviction that there is more to life than meets the eye, it would be foolish to take too much notice of secular people with short or non-existent historical memories who confidently predict its passing. Religion has provided people with a powerful impetus towards living lives of integrity; it has encouraged faith, hope and love to flourish in unlikely places; it has enabled people to see beyond surface realities to enduring truths, or so they have believed. If we do not have religion, then what would replace it? Marxism is one example of an alternative to religion that has proved to be a mere blip in history, even though twenty years ago many thought of it as an eternal or at least interminable phenomenon. Religion will probably yet see out its detractors.

Since it has been around for ever, or almost so, the real issue for serious-minded people is not whether we should have religion but, rather, what sort of religion we should have. Of course religion can be the plaything of the pompous, the politician, the pathetic and the para-noid; a force that encourages foolish dependence; an abuse. Marx and Freud had a point.[6] One of John Bowker's books about religions and belief in God in the contemporary world is entitled *Licensed Insanities*. It often does seem that religions are institutions for the mad, the sad and the bad, and should come with a health alert: 'Warning! This religion can seriously destroy your health; or somebody else's, if you follow it to the letter.' But it can be a life-enhancing force for good, helping people to glimpse the mystery of Transcendent truths that lie below the surface of this life.

IS AN INTERFAITH 'THEOLOGY OF RELIGIONS' DESIRABLE AND POSSIBLE?

An urgent current task is to attempt a theology of religions that can enable us to sound these depths that are far beneath life's superficialities. We need to be willing to accept that many people quite different from ourselves touch these depths because of their faith, not despite the fact that their faith is different in its range of commitments from ours. If so, then surely an interfaith theology of religions is urgently needed so that we can share the extraordinary resources that religions open up to their adherents.

In some ways, an emphasis upon theology is rather Christian. Judaism and Islam emphasize religious law, and Confucianism stresses ethics, to give examples of alternative emphases. But let us interpret theology to mean, 'What sort of Transcendence is Transcendence; what does what it requires of us infer about it?'

Most religions would have something important to say about this. Unfortunately, most theologies of religion have hitherto articulated a sectarian view of otherness. There are many writings from Christian, Muslim, Buddhist and Hindu points of view about attitudes towards other faiths. Many are judgemental, though some are not. Most suffer from the charge of special pleading and of failing to rejoice at the sheer variety of human responses to the Transcendent. The majority fail to see that such variety may mirror the myriad responses of Transcendence to human beings. Instead of such a sectarian enterprise, we need to look at the meaning of faith and religion together. The result would not be a liberal hotchpotch but a serious effort to understand, learn from and even appropriate insights from other perspectives that seem valuable but are missing or played down by one's own tradition of faith. And we would profit from pondering the responses others offer that, for one reason or another, we do not feel able to accept. Maybe also we shall find that we did not know as much about others' faith as they are able to tell us, or in ways that were truly significant.

Is such a quest possible? George Lindbeck and other scholars have enabled us to see how difficult it is for us to comprehend other systems of belief that have their own internal logic.[7] The fact that Jesus is located within Islamic and, to a lesser extent, Jewish and Hindu worlds of meaning as well as in Christianity illustrates this point. He is conformed to other perspectives so that Christians see him there, as it were, through a distorting mirror.[8] Yet this proves only the difficulty of the enterprise of any form of communication, not its impossibility. We must learn to be theologically and religiously multilingual. No doubt we shall always remain more at home within our own religion, as with our mother tongue, but it is not impossible to learn another's, if one has the humility to discern the limitations of one's understanding.

Has this interfaith quest for a theology of religions not already begun? The answer must be, to some extent, yes, it has. For the last twenty years of his life, Wilfred Cantwell Smith, who died in 2000, articulated the need and suggested a process for the pursuit of a world theology.[9] He was not exactly a lone voice in the wilderness. Among other practitioners, one could point to the Roman Catholic–Hindu scholar Raimon Panikkar, whose mixed Spanish and Indian, Roman Catholic and Hindu parentage has led him to a creative interfaith dialogue.[10] Furthermore, there is the exciting work of the Comparative Theology Project in North America, based in Boston, where Robert Neville and John Berthrong work and are significant participants.

Yet there are three reservations about the enterprise as it has so far been undertaken. First, some scholars often seem to be indulging primarily in an internal dialogue with their divided selves, rather than listening to other voices. Second, one could hope for a more positive response from places of higher education. In Britain, many departments of theology and religious studies are dominated by academics from the traditional Christian disciplines, with the occasional lecturer in another faith present as a minority voice. Even when scholars of different religions work together in university departments, does this lead to creative, fruitful and dialogical work or does each intellectual simply get on with their own specialist interests? The latter is often the case. Finally, even scholars who have surveyed the field of religious studies have often retreated into their own religion for theological reflection. For example, the British scholar Philip Meadows, now working in the USA, has written that 'inter-religious dialogue is a means and not an end in itself. It is the responsibility of dialogians to account for their new experiences in terms of their own worldview: a step in which a dialogian becomes a theologian.'[11] But is this really the case? This would certainly be true of a traditional Christian theologian (or a dialogian or dialogician of any religion); but in today's religiously diverse societies must one not have the imaginative and humane resources to go a step further? Meadows's is an ironic statement, since he draws on his background in computing and his knowledge of Hinduism to claim that 'Through immersion in, and interaction with, the thought world of the Hindu, made possible through inter-religious dialogue, one may attain to an understanding which approximates, really-but-not fully, that of the "full" insider.'[12] If that is the case, why would one then wish to retreat into one's own world to interpret another worldview, rather than attempt a joint interpretation that may lead both dialogicians further into the truth?

DOES FAITH GET IN THE WAY?

In North America, there is at present an odd and noisy debate about whether religious studies as a specialist field improperly privileges faith stances: for example, Donald Wiebe argues that such faith infects[13] the discourse of religious studies, which should be a scientific undertaking; he wants to marginalize the place of faith in the study of theology in seminaries.[14] He and his followers have pertinent things to say, and have a fine time debunking, sometimes fairly, the views of distinguished scholars like Mircea Eliade.[15] They are much indebted to the behavioural sciences for their critique, but do not seem to have similar misgivings about those disciplines' origins within regnant, assertive and naïvely self-confident nineteenth-century atheism and agnosticism.[16] Nor do they seem to know or have pondered how indebted early universities like al-Azhar, Cambridge and the Sorbonne were to a theological vision of a world in which divine knowledge was not an infection but was seen as a necessity for the cultured, erudite and perfectible person.

It is true that people are religious for a variety of reasons. A Muslim man in a Pakistani village might go to the mosque for Friday prayers because he has sincere faith. He might go, instead, out of habit and convention, or because of what people might say and do if he does not attend. The mosque is a useful place to meet many other men and to gossip, so he might look forward to prayers for that reason. In a society like Pakistan where religion and culture are still tightly interwoven, people may be sincerely religious, not because they possess deep personal faith in God but because Islam affects whom you can marry, what you can wear, your social status (if, for instance, you are a descendant of the Prophet Muhammad or if you have been on the annual pilgrimage to Mecca and Medina). Some people in such countries may take religion very seriously as social glue that cements people and customary practices together, and give at least lip service to conventional beliefs, but not be the sort of Muslim who is fiercely devoted to the teachings of God and his Prophet. Such people exist in all religions. Still, I have argued in *Religion: A Beginner's Guide* that

> I attach particular significance to the conviction that religion points to a phenomenon beyond itself and this mundane existence: to what theists would call God; though Buddhists and others would use other terminology ... It is by no means the case that even all religious people in the modern world believe in the phenomenon known (amongst other terms) as God or Transcendence ... I would certainly not call these sceptics irreligious, but I would contend that they miss religion's most important dimension and its greatest and most wondrous mystery.[17]

Whether readers agree with this or not, it remains the case that all religions, even if they do not affirm or require belief in a personal or impersonal God, believe that there is more to life than meets the eye. Their adherents have to look at or usually through the sense perceptions to a view or views of life that are taken on trust. Often they rely on scriptures or foundational religious figures to help them discern what otherwise we would find difficult or even impossible.

So religion does not open its treasures only to those who pursue a purely 'scientific' method. Like it or not, religion deals not only with human social and individual behaviour that is susceptible to the human sciences, but also with bizarre and supra-natural beliefs and actions and with claims to Transcendent knowledge. We need to take faith seriously as a factor in studying the religions of the world. This may be the faith commitment (or lack of it) of particular scholars, or of the faith of the people studied, or both of these. People must learn to be sceptical about claims or assumptions that scientific methodology is objective; it is as culturally conditioned and subjective or even prejudiced as faith stances. It is true that some people of faith cannot get out of the way of religious evidence that points in directions that they do not like. But that is also true of austere rationalists who use slippery terminology associated with 'science' and 'scientific' method as though that guaranteed their superior independence of thought. Not at all: good scholars of religion may have faith, or may not; likewise, bad scholars of religion.

Given the nature of religious claims about matters of ultimate importance, it would be odd to keep God out of religion, as though it were self-evidently true that the only human ideas about that concept which can be discussed are those that explain it away. John Bowker's book *The Sense of God*, based on his Wilde Lectures given at Oxford University in

1972, raised this issue many years ago. Its subtitle, 'Sociological, Anthropological and Psychological Approaches to the Origin of the Sense of God', describes its subject matter. Bowker argued that 'far from the disciplines we have been surveying dissolving the possible reality of reference in the term "God", they actually seem to demand a return to that possibility if sense is to be made of their own evidence'.[18] In his preface to the book's second edition, the author reflected on one of the arguments he had been keen to make, which was 'that religions are accumulated and shared responses to the limitations imposed on the project of human lives by conditions in the environments in which those lives are set'. He explained that

> religions are the consequence of somatic exploration and exegesis – exploration, that is, of what this body is capable of doing, of experiencing, of being and of becoming. In the course of these explorations, and sustained by the continuing exegesis, discoveries were made which enabled humans to transcend what Freud would have called 'their abject points of departure'.[19]

This leads Bowker to claim that religions are systems organized to code, protect and transmit verbal and non-verbal information that has been tested and tried through many generations, and have proved to be of worth. He claims that

> Religions are the resource and inspiration of virtually all the most enduring and value-laden human achievements (think only of the obvious, in art, architecture, music, dance, drama, agriculture, astronomy, poetry, ethics), quite apart from what they have secured in the interior experiences of the brain and in the designations of absolute value, culminating in God.[20]

Bowker notes that, in the course of centuries, religions have come to set different priorities from each other. He terms them 'divergent anthropologies – divergent accounts, that is, of what it is to be human'.[21] Bowker's work suggests that we should refrain from setting faith and scientific method against each other in the way of many nineteenth-century proponents of the human sciences. Perhaps we can put it this way: religions are anthropological constructs, the work of human art and artistry. Foolish, however, is the person who fails to allow that they may be porous to Transcendent grace. If religion is about what is more than meets the eye, nevertheless that 'more' has to reveal itself through the human body or through human creations. The old-fashioned notion that anthropology and other human sciences explain away God is clearly mis-taken. They provide the edifice within which Transcendence, if Tran-scendence exists, can effect her presence among people. So faith remains important as the conviction of many people, the majority of people in most times and places, that there is more to life than meets the eye.

A DIALOGICAL THEOLOGY

Since many people do look to religions for access to a Transcendent voice or voices, it seems reasonable to suppose that an interfaith theology of religions is not only possible but also desirable. My desire in this section is not to anticipate answers that an interfaith theology of religions might offer up to us, but rather to suggest the process by which provisional answers can be reached. In short, I suggest that, in the contemporary world, that process can most appropriately be done dialogically. Members of the religions need to begin to answer this question together, not separately. We need to discover the riches that people of other faiths have, as well as to share our own, for the good of humanity.

There are many religious people who disagree. Some think they have all the answers, or the key to them, so do not need to converse with others except, perhaps, to inform them of the truth. The renowned twen-tieth-century Protestant theologian, Karl Barth, met the great Sri Lankan Protestant evangelist, D.T. Niles, for the first time in 1935 – the year of the Nuremberg Laws, when Adolf Hitler imposed updated forms of many of the medieval anti-Semitic Christian canonical rules against German Jews.[22] This should remind us that unwillingness to meet people of other faiths often permits us to slander them ignorantly and to act on that slander with vile and inhumane actions. Still, Barth told Niles that 'Other religions are just unbelief.' Niles asked him how many Hindus he had met. Barth told him, 'None.' Niles then queried how he knew reli-gion was unbelief. Barth replied, 'A priori.' Niles concluded, 'I simply shook my head and smiled.'[23]

Some Christian theologians point out that the later Barth (he died in 1968) made more space for a positive assessment of non-Christian reli-gions. There have even been brave attempts by post-Barthian scholars to claim that his emphasis on the priority of revelation makes interfaith dialogue not only possible but also necessary in the contemporary world.[24] Garrett Green has illustrated how Barth can be useful for an open-ended theology of religions.[25] Yet this all sounds like special pleading. If, religiously, you wander within Barth's intellectual constructs to the exclusion of all others, he makes perfect sense. His logic is sometimes enthralling, his insights often brilliant; but why would one accept his presuppositions? He and his followers might argue, 'By faith.' Yet it seems an odd sort of faith in the Christian God of love that would marginalize the religious beliefs and practices of most humans. Professor Nicholas Lash of Cambridge University has been known to observe humorously in conversation that Barth wrote six million words to say, 'No!' Barth's view does, indeed, seem a negative view of the human religious enterprise from a very narrow, Protestant and exclusive perspective. As time goes by, his work seems more loquacious than long-lasting, understandable mostly as a reaction to a liberal theology that had little to say in the context of the evil of the First World War and the subsequent rise of fascism and Nazism. Ironically, Barth's theology itself now has little to say in its broad general thrust to an interconnected world of diverse religions and cultures. For all the occasional insights he offers, he seems to address a world we have lost.

Why would we believe Barth's hermetically sealed truth, rather than the hermetically sealed truth of a Muslim like Mawdudi (1904–1979), whose Jamaat i-Islami association has tried to popularize his updated form of traditional Sunni teaching in Pakistan, the United Kingdom and many other countries; or that of the exclusivist Hindu organization, the Rashtriya Svyamsevak Sangh (RSS), founded in the 1920s, and ideologues like its founder, K.B. Hedgewar, who suggest that India is for Hindus? There are lots of examples in the history of the world's religions of people who, in their own view, alone, or in the company of a few devotees, know the truth of things, or assert the fact that they do. The hermeneutics of suspicion is a useful tool for us to adopt towards them.

It seems reasonable to suppose that Transcendence may be telling us, within the processes of globalization, that we should be listening to each other. The age-old process of dialogue (a minority strand in past inter-religious relations, though nonetheless a definite element) should, in the contemporary world, come into its own. There are compelling reasons why we must listen to each other. Not the least is the fact that if we do not, then the ill-will generated by our sullen exclusivities in a planet that humans are capable of destroying will probably bring that destruction about.

TRAVELS WITH MY AUNT: DIALOGUE WITH OTHER RELIGIONS

In the autumn of 1992, the BBC World Service department sent me off to South Asia to make radio programmes, under the title *Gods, Guides and Gurus*, on the minority faiths of that region, excluding Hinduism and Islam. I spent eight weeks interviewing archbishops and patriarchs, monks and gurus, the disciples of living gods and dead intercessors, the rich and the poor, politicians and protestors, the wise and the learned (who are not always the same). Four years later, I made another series called *The Missionaries*. This entailed a four-week journey to South Africa, Tanzania, Kenya and Egypt. Then, later that year, I visited the USA. My purpose in those programmes was to examine how religions, old and new, renew themselves and adapt to new situations and circumstances. I was very grateful to the BBC for these opportunities to meet with people of many different faiths.

My partner in pilgrimage was David Craig, then executive producer of the BBC World Service's Religion Department. He and I devised these programmes. I learned much by talking with him about our experiences of meeting and interviewing many and diverse people. His partnership reminded me that any theological cogitation is a corporate exercise. If we are simply creatures of libraries, we live entirely in our own head. We come to our deepest knowledge of Transcendent reality through our relationships with others: by meeting, conversing and reflecting not only with dead and unknown people, however great, in reading their written words, but also with the living, with whom we have to share this planet now.

I learned much about dialogue from the process of interviewing. Anyone who makes the sort of programmes I did no doubt needs a range of communication skills, about which I am incompetent to comment. This is neither false modesty nor British reserve. I may have some modest talents in this area. For example, some of my interviewees told me that I have a seductive interviewing technique, as a result of which they told me things they had not meant to. What that technique is, I have no idea. If it is skill, it is not something I have ever learned or consciously adopted. I expect it arises out of my conviction that all dialogicians should aim to be humane.

As a student of religious studies, I see this humane quality as possessing three indispensable strands: knowledge, empathy and rootedness. Without a certain amount of knowledge of other ways of believing and behaving, an interviewer asks the wrong questions or else misunderstands the answers. Interviewers can never know everything about another faith, or even their own; sometimes they know very little indeed. Yet they need to know enough. Sometimes there is an interesting balance between their knowledge and ignorance, which can lead to a very good interview. For example, I much admire Buddhism but find it difficult to understand, existentially as much as academically, some of its answers to the human predicament. So before I asked a Buddhist woman academic in Sri Lanka to explain how the Buddha knew he had been enlightened and how Buddhists could recognize an enlightened being, I did not quite see how this could be. Her answer wonderfully helped me to see and understand what the Buddha and Buddhists discern about enlightenment: she told me it was 'like the unfolding of a flower'. I found that a remarkably suggestive simile, and was reminded of C.F.D. Moule's observation in his New Testament lectures long ago in Cambridge that understanding the parables of Jesus is like looking at a captionless cartoon: either you get the point or you do not; either you see or else you wander in the dark like a blind person. I helped that Buddhist woman produce that unforgettable image by asking the right question: I needed to know something in order to help her to assist my listeners and me to learn more. Once I had found out more, my heart and soul and mind were quickened into making connections that I could talk through with people of other faiths, to see if those links made any sense to them, and to perceive what associations they themselves made between what I and they separately believe.

The second indispensable quality is empathy for other ways than one's own of describing, apprehending and internalizing Transcendence. Empathy is not the capacity to believe nothing and so be intrigued by everything. Nor does it necessitate believing everything you are told. Both would be hopeless for programme makers, who have to choose what is important and critical for their programmes and have not the time to include the trivial, the completely wacky and the insignificant. I indicated in Chapter 2 that I am a Methodist Christian, an Arminian inclusivist and I thank God for my roots. That is the rock from which I am hewn, the perspective from which I see. But the fact that I believe what I believe does not mean that I cannot try to see through another's eyes, and interpret their ways of focusing faith and hope and love, or other Transcendent qualities. In fact, precisely because I believe what I do, I should attempt to see as others do. Also, as an interviewer,

I discovered that people open up their hearts to you – and reveal their private dreams publicly – not when you pretend to convictions you do not share, but when you seem to understand their views, or are genuinely trying to, and are fair minded in eliciting them.

A learned debate is going on at present about the limits or even possibility of an empathetic approach to other religions. This is largely a storm in a teacup, kept alive by the understandable need to censure a few pretentious scholars of religious studies who foolishly overestimate their ability to understand different ways of faith. They are far too certain of their capacity to be insiders.[26] Even if we marry into another culture, speak another language and try our best to empathize, can we really see as others see? We can aspire to, and get some way towards doing so. But foolish is the scholar who thinks he can easily and definitely categorize and place and comprehend another. It is also true that empathy is not enough. Shakespeare's character Iago is an empathetic figure. He insinuates himself into Othello's psyche, perfectly understands his strengths and weaknesses and takes advantage of them so as to destroy him and his wife, Desdemona. Ninian Smart's notion of informed and warm empathy is useful.[27] We must try to understand out of care for and accountability to others. Those who dislike the concept of empathy have the responsibility of suggesting an alternative way of attempting to understand others. When some maintain that we cannot, they are surely mistaken. It is unquestionably a mystery that and how humans communicate with each other, but we do; not wholly effectively, but sometimes wonderfully so.

The third essential quality is rootedness. I have mentioned my religious roots in Methodism. It always intrigues me how many Christian ecumenists of the 1960s and 1970s saw ecumenism as trading in their roots for a vision of an as yet chimerical united religious institution. Most people who wander the highways and byways of inter-religious dialogue know where they have come from. Pilgrims ought not to be obsessed by a myth of origins, but neither should they fail to pay attention to where Transcendence has placed or directed them. Besides, how parochial it is of such Christians in a world of rapid globalization to adopt a word, 'ecumenism', referring to the habitable earth, the inhabitants of earth or the whole human race[28] to indicate the Christian family of faith, and to assume that an obsession with institutional reformation is a visionary quest?

So the process of interviewing for radio programmes raised dialogical issues about knowledge, empathy and rootedness. These issues, age old, can often seem overwhelmingly new and fresh in a world of global communications and widespread religious emigration. In making *The Missionaries*, David and I wanted to ask how religions survive, develop and flourish when their adherents move to new places. Sometimes the religions do not endure. The Jews of India are a tragic example of how developments elsewhere in the faith can adversely affect the future of certain members of the religion. Because of emigration to Israel and elsewhere since the creation of independent India and Israel a year apart in 1947 and 1948, the number of Jews in South Asia seems now in irreversible decline. Also, racism in Israel has meant that many Indian Jews emigrated again to Canada and other countries. Some now wish they had stayed put in a country where they were often respected and well treated, and never persecuted.

Still, it was fascinating to hear how Judaism has flourished elsewhere, and how the recent Hindu and Muslim diasporas, among many others, have also embedded religions in new places that cause them to adapt in significant ways from their character in their ancient heartlands.

A CASE STUDY FOR DIALOGUE: DISCOVERING GOD WITH LATTER DAY SAINTS

Here I offer a brief review of my experiences with one interesting group with whom I spoke. These are the Latter Day Saints, who broke away from mainstream Christianity in the nineteenth century. They are often incorrectly called 'Mormons' after the *Book of Mormon*, which, with the King James Bible, is their authoritative scripture. They prefer to be called 'Saints'. Their headquarters is at Salt Lake City, Utah, the so-called 'Zion in the Mountains' where, after much persecution and the death of their founder, Joseph Smith, the early pioneers arrived in 1848.

Outsiders often know three things about Latter Day Saints: they practised polygamy; they baptize the dead; and they send young people to convert others. So I asked especially about these three areas. The director of area relations in the Public Service Department of this church told me that, although plural marriage was introduced by special revelation in 1843, it was rescinded in 1890 and is practised today by only a few Saints.

The reason why baptism is performed on behalf of the dead is because of the central importance of the family to the Saints. They believe that the extended family is linked through time and eternity and so baptism is a rite performed for those family members who, in their lifetimes, were not able or did not choose to become Saints. The managing director of the Family History Department in Salt Lake City told me that baptism on behalf of the dead is handled in ways that are sensitive to feelings of those who are not Latter Day Saints. Rites are conducted in the Temple in Salt Lake City. A living individual stands in place of the ancestor or ancestors. This ceremony is done in faithfulness to the commandment of Jesus that 'All must be born again.' The effectiveness of the sacrament is dependent upon the willingness of the dead person to accept it and to obey God's rules.

The theological justification for baptizing the dead is based on 1 Peter 3:18–22. I was told that the Saints' unique doctrine of these verses shows that they take this scripture passage more seriously than other Christians have. It was put to me in the following way. Christ talked of preaching to the spirits in prison. They need to hear the gospel and will do so in the next life, in which they will retain the choice of responding or not.

As early as 1894 the Saints kept records of family members and now they are computerized. Anyone is welcome to go to the archives and trace their ancestry. So it is not just Saints who turn up to find out whom they should baptize. Outsiders come to create their own family tree, for whatever reasons impel them to do so.

Most of the church's missionaries are young men and women between the ages of nineteen and twenty-three. At that time (1995), nearly fifty thousand Saints were serving missions in ninety-eight countries. The *Book of Mormon* was available in over eighty translations. All missionaries go out two by two, and rely on their own savings or family support for their mission period of eighteen months to two years. More than half of young Saints become missionaries. It is not exactly compulsory, but most do it. They apply to headquarters and are directed to a destination. One interviewee, now high up in the hierarchy, went to Japan for twenty-two months, after two months' language preparation in Hawaii. He said that lots of Saints pick up languages very easily, and put it down to their commitment to the cause.

I interviewed two young missionaries who were working on Temple Square. It was mid December, way below freezing, but they smiled away, telling me that their day starts at 6.30 a.m. When I asked one if it wasn't all a bit of a chore, she replied, 'Absolutely not. In my life, when I have given the Lord a crust, he gives us a loaf.' About three-quarters of the missionaries come from the USA, but things are changing.

I could have got the information I have just imparted to you from books.[29] What difference does dialogue make? Well, the enormous, almost unnerving verve of every Latter Day Saint to whom I spoke was extraordinary. The early Methodists were accused of being enthusiasts, but rarely have I been so conscious of and amused by my English reserve. Their ebullience made recording them fun as well as profitable.

It is clear that the Latter Day Saints are not mainstream Christians. For a start, they add the *Book of Mormon* to a particular and outdated translation of the Bible as revelation, and their biblical interpretation is idiosyncratic. Theologically, most Christians have dismissed them as a sect or even a cult, and called them 'Mormons', a designation they have not chosen for themselves. This reminded me that the word 'Christian' was bestowed, unasked for, upon members of a Jewish 'sect' or, less judgmentally, 'interpretative subgroup'.

In the modern world, it is better to converse with such a group than to marginalize it. Christians could engage in such conversation on the pragmatic grounds that the Saints are growing apace, and you ought to know the nature of your opposition! In 1947 their church had one million members and in 1963 two million. Now there are over nine million Saints, many in Africa and the Pacific islands. But there are sounder and more humane reasons for such conversation. The Saints may hold views that outsiders would regard as bizarre and misguided, but they have a deeply serious take on faith as human commitment to Transcendence and to other people. Kenneth Cracknell has written of the need to promote 'justice, courtesy and love'.[30] It ill-behoves religious people to act dishonourably and dismissively towards others.

Here are three positive reasons why it would be worthwhile for people of other faiths (including other Christians) to dialogue with the Latter Day Saints. First, the history of the Saints illustrates the sociological dimension of religion. I have already argued in this chapter that scholars and students of religion must take faith seriously and that the interpretations of those influenced by certain naïve ways of reading the human sciences that exclude faith are excessively and misleadingly reductionist. Yet anyone who teaches courses on religion to students doing theology and religious studies, still more to students training to be clergy, will know how obsessed many are with faith and religion as a twofold form of disembodied reality ('unreality' would be a better word), negotiating with a sacred text and a tradition that somehow happened outside time and space and thus teaches unchanging, uncontextualized truths. The problem with this sort of approach is that, in practice, scriptural passages or great religious teachers are made to justify graceless and implausible abuses as eternal verities. The practice of slavery, the oppression of women and gays, anti-Semitism and many other disastrous things have all been legitimated by this odd form of philosophical idealism masquerading as commitment to scriptural truth. Sometimes they still are. A dose of social theory applied to religion would help people of faith to dialogue in recognition that they are boundaried by time, geography and a host of other things. Thus, they should recognize how great a mystery is the truth that possesses them, and be open to see it elsewhere. The great mythic history of the trek to Utah, with its social consequences of polygamy and the creation in the early Saints of a certainty of being chosen by God for valorous and superhuman deeds, reminds us that religions, whatever else they are and convey, are social constructs.

Second, there are issues of truth to discuss and refine. It is relatively easy for any outsider to a system to see its little peculiarities and its large eccentricities. The context of dialogue allows one to ask searching questions about them, so long as you are willing to permit queries about your own faith's seeming oddities. I asked some Saints whom I interviewed about the specific importance of the King James Bible and whether the passage from 1 Peter could really mean what they take it to. Without a doubt, many disagreements between religions are enormous. This is why certain otherwise attractive pluralist philosophies like those of Radhakrishnan and John Hick should be treated with respectful wariness: they are less pluralist and more socially constrained than their proponents aver, and are also implausible in the face of such dissimilarity.

Finally, the Saints remind us of the passionate desire of many religious people to pass on to others what they have experienced of Transcendent reality in their lives, in the form in which they received it. In this period of globalization and religious diasporas, there is no diminution in the desire of religions to be missionary in their impetus. Even some traditionally non-missionary religions now get in on this act. First-generation Hindus in Chicago and Leicester not only seek to adapt and pass on their faith to their youngsters in the situation they find themselves, but also tell their stories to interested and truth-seeking outsiders. There are countless other examples of this phenomenon. What we need in a religiously plural world is not a moratorium on mission, which would turn us all into King Canutes vainly seated in front of the stormy ocean and telling the incoming waves to go back. Rather, we need to establish an ethic for disagreement. A particular problem is that too many religious people think they and other like-minded people alone have the truth, and that everybody else is culpably blind and so deserves to be treated badly. I suspect that this sense of superiority is a natural and mild form of paranoia in many humans, not least many secularists. Dialogue gives a context in which this kind of passionate commitment needs to be argued for and tested, not simply asserted and imposed.

THE LIMITS OF DIALOGUE

Are there limits to dialogue? In this section, I raise three important matters. Would an inter-religious dialogue be only for scholars? Should such dialogue avoid contentious theological issues and concentrate instead on matters of social justice, ethical endeavour and the like? Are there people with whom one ought not to dialogue?

There is a great need for religious scholars to put their knowledge at the service of studying the many and various ways of faith. Yet this should not be to the exclusion of other ways of creating an inter-religious way of learning about Transcendence. Indeed, it is not only desirable but also possible for the vast majority of non-specialists in the field of religious studies to engage in transforming interfaith dialogue.

Let us take, for example, a Christian church and a Hindu temple in a mixed society. When I worked in inner city Leicester, every Christmas time the Christian congregation invited local Hindus to a carol service. We sang, read from the Bible, preached a sermon (translated into Gujerati) and afterwards drank tea and ate vegetarian mince pies. The act of Christian worship was not dumbed down, but neither were Hindu friends seen as evangelistic targets. We talked of the good news of God's incarnation in Christ. On other occasions, we went to *puja* in the local Hindu temple. Good discussion usually happened over refreshments in both places of worship: what was the difference and what were the similarities between Hindu convictions of the downcoming (*ava-tri*) of God in many times and places, and the Christian insistence that Christ's incarnation was once and for all. People also mentioned how much a belief that God's coming in personal form meant to them. Had Muslims and Jews, still more Confucianists and Buddhists, joined the conversation, it would have been even more fascinating and contentious. Disagreements were possible because people genuinely enjoyed and valued being with each other.

It is striking that on such an occasion ordinary Hindus and Christians talked about God; in other words, they did theology together. Many lived close by each other in the neighbourhood. Hindus would invite Christian friends to weddings and funerals and other religious events, and *vice versa*. This would lead to discussions about the nature of God. I contrast this with many inter-religious academic conferences at which learned scholars would often say that theology is a poor basis for discussion among people of different faiths and it is better to concentrate on matters of ethics and social responsibility. Why do scholars of theology find inter-religious theologizing difficult or impossible, but not ordinary people? Maybe scholars are obsessed by minutiae and see all the problems of mutual understanding. Even so, most ordinary people seem to know that God is important in religion and want to talk about that subject. They seem to have grasped an important point.

Many religions have identified groups with whom they should not talk. Many mainstream Christians would shun conversation with Latter Day Saints (or Jehovah's Witnesses and other marginal groups), on the grounds that they distort the true meaning of Christianity and so are inadequate representatives of that faith. Sunni Muslims have sometimes found it hard to speak kindly of and with Shia' Muslims, and both groups are suspicious of members of heterodox Islamic groups like the Ahmadiyya movements. If you apply widely the convictions I expressed above about the need for Christians and others to dialogue with Latter Day Saints, then, *mutatis mutandis*, it would seem best, in a religiously diverse world, for people to speak with groups towards whom they have traditionally been hostile, rather than shun them. Only by talking can we refine our differences, locate them fairly and ask what we can do about them. We may end up by respecting the other rather than ignoring or even maligning them, even if we cannot hope to agree. But surprising things happen in dialogue, and it may be that agreement is more possible over a range of issues than we first thought.

To be sure, one can point to many reprehensible practices done in the name of religion. Why would one talk to someone who adopts a racist or fascist policy on religious grounds? Except that it might be worth the effort to try to change their minds rather than leave them in ignorance. So it is a mistake to avoid contact with others on the grounds of their impure faith, doctrine and actions. Such avoidance might also be a device to stop us from hearing strong objections to our own flawed positions.

Many politicians express things in ways that perfectly illustrate the pointlessness of some dialogue. They often adopt a strategy of appearing omnicompetent, while negotiating privately with those who have other things to tell, but religious people should not follow that flawed device. Dialogue requires participants who hear, who genuinely listen to each other. So the major occasion when it seems pointless to converse with someone is when that person has no intention of listening, only pronouncing. I have been in a number of mosques, churches and other places of worship and talked to people whom I have resolved never to meet again on the grounds that it is a waste of time. Occasionally, I have found the courage to tell them why and to express my conviction that they would not be adequate spokesmen (since they usually are men) for their deep-rooted convictions until they test them against other views and allow others to ask questions and even voice objections. Occasionally, I have had my own prejudices questioned. For example, when I have talked at home with door-to-door salesmen and saleswomen of their faith, I have often shown them out as quickly as possible. They had one line, it was a hard sell and they had not learned to take notice of any queries asked about it. Now and again, however, I have had interesting and fruitful conversations. For example, I have been told of the personal devotions of a Jehovah's Witness, and been prayed over by a member of a heterodox black church who genuinely wanted to locate where God's Spirit was in my vision of reality. What a pity not to have been enriched by such encounters because of a prior conviction that they are too time consuming or always lead to one-sided monologues.

AN INTER-RELIGIOUS DIALOGICAL THEOLOGY OF RELIGIONS

What might the result of such an inter-religious dialogical theology of religions look like? Well, it will not issue in a single world religion, either a present one that will win out over all comers, or a new inclusive one that will capture the hearts, souls and minds of humankind. Globalization is not a process that will lead to monochrome mediocrity, still less uniform excellence. Humans are exasperatingly and delightfully varied, perversely pluriform in character and conviction, and will no doubt remain so.

In our religiously plural world, some people prefer co-existence and respect between the religions as preferable to a takeover bid by one against the others. On their side they would seem to have common sense and the fact of simple observation that most religious people are content to stay put where they are. Then there are those people who break away from one religion to form their own. Often they do not mean to, just as early Christians proposed an eccentric interpretation of Judaism and may have been rather surprised that they pulled off a brand new religion instead. There are also people who sincerely feel that they must transfer their allegiance from one faith to another, since the adopted faith is closer to the truth as they perceive it and as it enfolds them.

There are also, however, growing numbers of people who partake in beliefs and practices of more than one faith. They have been described as people with hyphenated identities or who are involved in multiple religious participation; we shall develop this point in Chapter 5. Their critics make old-fashioned jibes about syncretism but rather miss the point that most religions have been overtly syncretistic and have greatly flourished thereby. But people have implicitly seen the point that, if you lack what the other possesses, it is a good idea to borrow from it.

Some religious people do not simply borrow from other faiths because it seems a good idea to do so. They are willy-nilly caught between different worlds of faith. In China, for instance, over long centuries many people have partaken in the religious practices of more than one faith. Increasingly this now happens in other parts of the world. Picture, for example, the American children of a Jewish and a Christian parent. Orthodox Jewish belief denotes Jewish identity through the mother. What, however, if the father is the Jew and yet both parents bring up the children to identify with Judaism, not Christianity? It might be thought: so much the worse for them, since what religions have long believed to be the case will not change to accommodate new situations. In fact, though religions are conservative institutions, they are not utterly inflexible. Orthodox Jewish law may have to develop new strategies to take account of new possibilities in the contemporary world. It would be an irony, indeed, if an unbendable Jewish orthodoxy brought about the decline and demise of Judaism, when all Hitler's efforts failed.

Another example could be of a Parsi man who converts to Christianity yet retains a strong memory of his grandmother's saintly life, which was goodly and godly because of, not despite, her Parsi religion. So he has no desire to utterly reject his religious past. He strives to hold together in some kind of creative tension what he was with what he has become. Traditional exclusive interpretations of Christian faith are of no use in helping him to do this.

Religious people may have to be bold enough to insist that old interpretations, fit for another sort of world, may have to change, rather than exclude such products of our global village as eccentric or unacceptable. Although all religions warn their adherents of the dangers of conforming to passing fads and fancies rather than relying upon ancient truth, they have also to make sense of and be relevant to each generation. It may be hard but it is not impossible to distinguish between the ersatz and the genuine seeker after truth. Both examples I have offered involve people who, in a world of increasing complexity and choice, sincerely wish to make a committed choice – but one that raises problems that religions have hitherto hardly had to deal with. If people of faith believe that religions can be both human constructs and channels for Transcendent grace, it ought not to be beyond the wit of humans to bring about an appropriate *aggiornamento* or updating of religion for the present age, so that it can more effectively mediate Transcendence. The reforms of the Second Vatican Council (1958–1965) began this process in the Roman Catholic Church, which has been radically reshaped and reformed more than once before. Most religions have transformed themselves over time, sometimes very greatly indeed and on a number of occasions, in order to take account of the world as it is rather than as it was – actually or in the light of past ideals that later seem misplaced.

What is more important than offering crystal-ball predictions about the consequences and outcomes of an inter-religious dialogical theology of religions is to commend its pursuit as of vital importance in the contemporary world. Religious people must talk to each other rather than stay apart; and converse about important issues, not anodyne inconsequentialities. In a speech in Washington on 26 June 1954, Winston Churchill observed that 'To jaw-jaw is better than to war-war.' A low-level justification of an inter-religious dialogical theology of religions would accept this conviction as at least a start. In truth, we need more. Real dialogue is about them and us becoming we – we asking together: what does Transcendence want of her human children? The answers will be varied, but such a dialogue is essential for mutual respect and learning, the survival of this planet, and the enrichment of the heart and mind and soul. Because religions have so often marginalized the other, who is seen as different and inferior, dialogue becomes a way of seeing them as human and faithful. Dialogue can therefore lead to the mending of difficult, even utterly broken, relationships. An example of this repairing of a fractured association can be found in the extraordinary modern growth in Jewish–Christian relations, to which we now turn.

4 TO MEND THE WORLD

IS TOLERANCE ENOUGH?

When the Christian churches began to take inter-religious dialogue seriously, from the 1960s onwards, there was a tendency to engage in multilateral dialogue, to treat all relationships as though they were the same. For some years (full-time from 1988 to 1995) I was secretary of the British Methodist Church's Committee for Relations with People of Other Faiths. I already knew, and had my knowledge much reinforced during that period, that relations with, for example, Buddhists raised, in certain respects, profoundly different issues from those raised from relations with Zoroastrians. For many years church officials were reluctant to engage in bilateral dialogue, which Jewish–Christian dialogue exemplifies.

This chapter explores the importance of both bilateral and multilateral dialogue, mainly at official levels in religious organizations. It proposes that Jewish–Christian dialogue has much to offer other forms of bilateral and multilateral dialogue. It also suggests that Jewish–Christian relations may benefit from being mapped on a wider map of interfaith encounter. To justify this contention, I shall examine four important issues raised by this particular dialogue. Since most of my experience has been in the British scene, I will concentrate on this region – to indicate why and how such a dialogue began and has been sustained.

There is one necessary caveat to make. Much extraordinary inter-religious dialogue has been done at unofficial levels by ordinary members of different faiths. Too many works on dialogue give the impression that quality relations between members of different faiths occur only between religious bureaucrats or scholars. In this book I have tried to indicate that this is not so. Still, without the blessing of the official organs of their religion, members of some religions (not least those with strong central organizations, like many Christian churches and Jewish and to a lesser degree Muslim groups) are hampered in their ground-breaking dialogical work by suspicions that they are letting the side down. (I shall give a specific example below of how my own denomination has recognized this and sought to overcome it.) Hence, it is foolish to argue that religious structures can be ignored or bypassed. They are far from the only participants in dialogue, and their dialogue, like those of some scholars, is often more theoretical than practical. But the importance of engaging official religious bodies in dialogue is very great, as we shall see in the rest of this chapter.

We begin with what may fancifully be regarded as a parable of inter-religious relationships. In the eighteenth century, French Protestant Huguenots, escaping from persecution in their homeland, built a church in Brick Lane in London's East End. They made good in their new situation, moved to other localities and sold their church to a Methodist group. The latter too, by dint of hard work, improved their economic situation, and moved to less deprived areas. They sold the church to Jews fleeing persecution in mainland Europe, who turned it into a synagogue. In their turn, the Jews flourished and moved to Hampstead in north London. Now, the same building is in the hands of Muslims from a poor rural area of Bangladesh. So far, this place of worship has heard prayers offered in French, English, Hebrew and Arabic. It is fascinating to speculate: what next for this remarkable building? One hopes that, if its Bengali worshippers make good and move on, it will remain a holy place, a parable of religious diversity in the contemporary world.[1]

If this is a parable, it is one that has a difficult as well as a positive message. It is gratifying, even heart warming, to note that different religious groups have felt comfortable about selling a treasured and hallowed property to other religious groups. Maybe each departing congregation has preferred to sell its sacred property to those who pray differently, but at least pray, rather than to a purchaser who would use it for purely material purposes. Still, this form of goodwill towards members of other faith groups, if such it be, is of limited significance. What interaction did Huguenots, Methodists, Jews and Muslims actually have? Probably not much. One can commend a generalized and mild form of generosity by one religious group towards another without thinking that such benevolence is enough for our increasingly inter-linked world.

The appalling fate of Jews in mainland Europe in the twentieth century illustrates that the apparent tolerance of religious groups towards others cannot withstand the machinations of evil people working to convince otherwise well-meaning people of the truth of age-old, often deep-seated and unconscious prejudices that justify the marginalization and even persecution and murder of the outsider. Jewish–Christian relations have had a particular urgency since the dark years of the Second World War. In the United Kingdom, the Council of Christians and Jews (CCJ) was founded in 1942, as news came of the death camps in mainland Europe. A decision on 20 March 1942 brought the CCJ into being. A resolution proposed

> That since the Nazi attack on Jewry has revealed that anti-semitism is part of a general and comprehensive attack on Christianity and Judaism and on the ethical principles common to both religions which form the basis of the free national life of Great Britain the Council adopts the following aims:
>
> (a) To check and combat religious and racial intolerance.
>
> (b) To promote mutual understanding and goodwill between Christians and Jews in all sections of the community, especially in connection with Problems arising from conditions created by the war.
>
> (c) To promote fellowship between Christian and Jewish youth organizations in educational and cultural activities.
>
> (d) To foster co-operation of Christians and Jews in study and service directed to post-war reconstruction.[2]

Of the important themes that emerge from the resolution of the newly formed CCJ, two have become very significant in Jewish–Christian relations: the emphases upon education and upon anti-Semitism. The CCJ was nearly sunk before it floated by Dr Hertz, the Chief Rabbi, largely because of its educational strategy. He objected to two things. First, he insisted that Jews and Christians should not interfere in the other's teaching and he reckoned that part of the CCJ's educational work breached that principle. He also claimed that Orthodox Jews were inadequately represented on the CCJ Executive.[3] Matters were patched up but the issues raised by CCJ's foundation have cast long shadows on Jewish–Christian relations.

The deepest issues are fourfold. Does a civilized land like the UK really need to deal with anti-Semitism? Are institutional Jewish–Christian relations at the mercy of internal religious angst and self-definition? What form of education is necessary and acceptable in order to improve Jewish–Christian relations? As wicked as anti-Semitism was and remains, is it still an adequate reason for the existence Jewish–Christian relations? In the remainder of this chapter, we shall deal with these issues.

ANTI-SEMITISM IN PRACTICE

Despite the United Kingdom's sometimes self-serving reputation for sheltering refugees from foreign oppression, such liberality of action has only recently been matched, at least to some extent, by a generosity of spirit and its enshrinement in legislation. The work of the Council of Christians and Jews needed not only to draw attention to dark bigotry and foul acts in other countries, but also to challenge British xenophobia and anti-Semitism.

British prejudice and concomitant hatred of Jews go back centuries. The Jews were expelled in 1290 by the Plantaganet King Edward I, the first expulsion of all Jews from any European country in the medieval period. They were permitted back during Oliver Cromwell's Protectorate in 1656; grudgingly, not for reasons of natural justice but because Cromwell believed Jews could renew England's trade as, in his opinion, they had helped the economic growth of Amsterdam and other mainland European cities, especially ports. Full emancipation did not occur until the second half of the nineteenth century. Baron de Rothschild took his seat in the House of Commons on 26 July 1858. It was the fourth time he had been elected as the representative of the City of London, but he was forbidden from taking his place as an MP because he would not take the oath of allegiance in the time-honoured Christian way. He was not a particularly active Member of Parliament; he is not recorded as ever having made a speech in the House of Commons. A more important marking post in the integration of Jews into national life was probably when Gladstone made Sir George Jessel Solicitor-General in 1871; he was the first Jew to become a Minister of the Crown. Three years earlier, Benjamin Disraeli, a Christian of Jewish origin, had briefly become Prime Minister; he served as Prime Minister for a second, longer period from 1874 to 1880.[4]

The CCJ had precursors in Britain who sought to improve Jewish–Christian relations. The London Society for the Study of Religions was founded in 1904. It has been a forum for scholarly debate, and has included Jews since its foundation. The London Society for Jews and Christians (LSJC) was formed in 1927. It organizes regular discussions and debates between Jews and Christians of different persuasions. It has an annual garden party in Westminster Abbey's grounds, and a lecture in Church House, the Church of England's administrative headquarters. It seeks to understand how both religions are practised as well as what they believe. There have been joint celebrations of Hanukkah and Christmas. Every other year there is a Model Seder, to which Christians are invited.[5] The LSJC has aimed to increase religious understanding and mutual respect for differences of faith and practice, and has sought to combat religious intolerance.[6]

The work of dedicated individuals is also noteworthy. James Parkes (1896–1981), an Anglican clergyman, became aware of anti-Semitism when he went to work in Geneva in 1928. He was one of the first Christians to recognize that the origins of anti-Semitism were partly in the teaching of the churches, from the early church fathers onwards. He argued this in his doctoral thesis of 1934. He was put on Hitler's list of people to be eliminated. When he retired in 1966, he gave his library to Southampton University. We have the benefit of his autobiography.[7]

Subterranean and implicit anti-Semitism is often as shocking and as revealing as its straightforward forms. Some of English literature's most influential descriptions of Jews have arisen out of ignorance and prejudice: Shakespeare's depiction of Shylock in *The Merchant of Venice* was written at a time when any Jew in England was illegally present and could expect exposure and death; and Charles Dickens's distressing caricature of Fagin in his novel *Oliver Twist* makes sense against a background of continuing mid-Victorian anti-Semitism, which spilled over into later times.

For example, many authors of popular British twentieth-century literature demonstrate a reflex anti-Semitism. A noteworthy example of such unthinking prejudice is Agatha Christie, the so-called 'Queen of Crime', whose publishers declare her to be the world's best-selling novelist, writing works that have been translated into every major language. In her *Three Act Tragedy*, first published in 1935, Mr Satterthwaite, an elderly snob yet acute observer of the human condition, contemplates a young man named Oliver Manders:

> A handsome young fellow, twenty-five at a guess. Something, perhaps, a
> little sleek about his good looks. Something else – something – was it
> foreign? Something unEnglish about him ...
>> Egg Lytton Gore's voice rang out:
>> 'Oliver, you slippery Shylock —'
>> 'Of course,' thought Mr. Satterthwaite, 'that's it – not foreign – Jew!'[8]

Actually, the great Belgian detective, Hercule Poirot, is benevolently disposed towards the young man, who gets his girl in the end. But that book
was published the same year as the Nazis enacted the Nuremberg Laws to
deprive German Jews of the ordinary rights of citizens. Christie used
barbed language about Jews in many more of her works. The point is not
that she was a particularly virulent exponent of anti-Semitism, or even
consciously anti-Jewish. Worse in a way, her casual comments illustrate the
stereotypes widespread in British society of her day. To be fair, while at an
archaeological dig in Iraq with her husband, Max Mallowen, she encoun-
tered the German director of antiquities in Baghdad, one Dr Jordan, whom
she thought at first to be gentle and considerate, though she later discovered him to be a spy as well as an anti-Semite. She recorded:

> Then there was a mention by someone, quite casually, of Jews. His face
> changed; changed in an extraordinary way that I had never noticed on
> anyone's face before.
> He said: 'You do not understand. Our Jews are perhaps different from
> yours. They are a danger. They should be exterminated. Nothing else will
> really do but that.'
> I stared at him unbelievingly. He meant it. It was the first time I had
> come across any hint of what was to come later from Germany. People
> who travelled there were, I suppose, already realizing it at that time, but
> for ordinary people, in 1932 and 1933, there was a complete lack of
> foreknowledge.[9]

At about the same time as she wrote *Three Act Tragedy*, a little after the
above incident, Dame Agatha could write, 'He's a Jew, of course, but a
frightfully decent one.'[10] One of her most perceptive yet appreciative
critics notes that her offensive remarks against Jews mostly cease from
this time. In later books her references to Jews and their critics are part
of one of her most nimble sleights of hand: to use readers' bigotry against
them so as to mislead them.

 Still, there is no evidence that Christie ever expressed embarrassment
at her unthinking acceptance of anti-Semitism. Nor did she question the
appropriateness of using her readers' intolerance as a part of her strategy

to bamboozle and misdirect them. In a world of Holocaust and genocide, she missed the point of her own deception by deep-rooted societal antipathies, nurtured by her deep Christian faith. Christie was a creature of her time and location; others saw the point more clearly than she did, but some never observed it even as naïvely as she did.

We need an educative process that seeks to help religious people not simply to tolerate but also to rejoice in the otherness of the other, a process that regards diversity as of Transcendent value rather than the result of human sin or ignorance.

INSTITUTIONAL JEWISH–CHRISTIAN RELATIONS

We have already mentioned the creation of the Council of Christians and Jews in the United Kingdom. We turn now to the question: are institutional Jewish–Christian relations at the mercy of internal religious angst and self-definition? We have seen how the Chief Rabbi nearly withdrew Orthodox Jewish support from CCJ just after it was founded. In November 1954, Cardinal Griffin withdrew as president on orders from Rome, arguing that 'in the educational field ... the promotion of mutual understanding is being conducted in a way likely to produce religious indifferentism'. Several articles in *Common Ground*, the CCJ journal, were accused of promoting this point of view. In particular, one by Arnold Toynbee was mentioned, in which he argued, movingly but perhaps not convincingly, that

> In reality mankind has never been divided into an elect minority monopolizing the light of God's countenance and a gentile majority sitting in outer darkness. There has never been any supernaturally privileged inner circle within the human family. The only treatment of history that is objective is one that treats all communities as equals; and this objective view of history is the only view that we can afford to present to our children in our now rapidly shrinking world.[11]

Other Roman Catholics than the cardinal also withdrew until the *aggiornamento* (updating) of the Second Vatican Council, begun in Pope John XXIII's pontificate (1958–1963), permitted a return of Roman Catholic voices to the inner circles of the CCJ.

Such institutional brinkmanship is always a problem for organizations that promote Jewish–Christian relations which are dependent, at least to some extent, upon the favour of official bodies in either religion. The unwise words of the British Commonwealth's Chief Rabbi Jonathan

Sacks in the wake of the death of the much loved and non-Orthodox Jewish Rabbi Hugo Gryn, in which he seemed to imply that Gryn was not a Jew and had caused others to stumble, successfully led to calls in the British Jewish community for non-Orthodox Jewish presidents of CCJ. Until recently, the Chief Rabbi was the only Jewish president, though Christians were represented by the Archbishops of Canterbury and Westminster and the Moderator of the Free Church Federal Council. Also, despite Pope John Paul II's remarkable advocacy of positive Jewish–Christians relations, his papacy has recently been dogged by disjointed and equivocal actions that cause outsiders to ponder the consistency of Roman Catholic teaching about other ways of faith. Was the Pope's position most clearly seen in his Universal Prayer of 12 March 2000, asking for forgiveness for sins against the Jewish people and other groups? Or is it seen in his attempt in the Vatican document *Dominus Iesus*, published on 6 August 2000, to resurrect traditional teaching that the Roman Catholic Church alone embodies the truth, noting, as it does, that other religions result from a purely human quest for God?[12] This bewildering ambivalence illustrates how factions fight for the victory of their point of view in the twilight years of stricken leaders. It does little to improve Jewish–Roman Catholic relations.

Institutional dialogue is fraught with perils – at the mercy of internal rifts and manoeuvrings for power and influence. There is always the temptation to abandon it in favour of grassroots dialogue: official bodies are mostly conservative in their stance and have their share of prima donnas struggling for personal influence rather than the common good. But the recent history of Jewish–Christian relations has shown how important institutional dialogue is. Without the official endorsement of their faith communities, individuals of goodwill are always open to charges of betrayal of the community and of godless innovation. There has been little if any attempt by the Ancient Orthodox churches of the East to reformulate teaching about Jews. As a result, anti-Semitism not only flourishes in Russia and other countries where this form of Christianity is present, but is condoned or even justified by the church hierarchy; whereas the Protestant Churches and especially the Roman Catholic Church have been transformed by institutional statements. These have liberated individuals to engage in dialogue as an officially endorsed enterprise of goodwill and Transcendent hope.

The seminal post-war document was *Nostra Aetate*, issued on 28 October 1965 in the pontificate of Paul VI, though it had its origins in his predecessor's deepest concerns and his, John XXIII's, summoning of a council to update the church's teaching on a wide range of issues. *Nostra Aetate* marked a great leap forward in Jewish–Roman Catholic relations. It declared that the church had her origins in ancient Israel, upon which she is dependent for her teaching, life and worship. So Catholics must not teach that God has rejected the Jews, nor that God and Christians should teach contempt for or hatred of them.[13] Hitherto, the official teaching of the church had portrayed the Jews as a deicide people, killers of God, who were therefore abandoned and rejected by him. Note, for example, the bowed, broken and humiliated images of Jews on cathedrals of medieval Europe, such as Notre Dame in Paris, begun in 1163, and Strassburg, mostly dating from the end of the twelfth century onwards, which had encouraged illiterate worshippers – who learned church teaching from such artefacts – to shun and loathe Jews.[14] It has taken many years since 1965 for the Roman Catholic Church to face up to some of the worst aspects of its history. *Nostra Aetate* makes no mention of the church's grave complicity in the history of Christian contempt for Jews. Indeed, Pope John, who was greatly influenced by the French Jew, Jules Isaac, who had coined the phrase about the churches 'teaching of contempt' for Jews, had wanted a statement made that dealt specifically with relations with the Jews. In the end, he had to accept one that also included other religions and referred to relations with the Jews for only two-fifths of its length.[15] The Vatican recognized the state of Israel only in 1994. A series of further statements has continued to update attitudes towards Jews; for example, in dealing with anti-Semitism in the liturgy, the catechism and other teaching. Despite certain hiccups in the progress, and the understandable desire of many Jews that the church should move more quickly and radically in updating its teaching, Jewish–Roman Catholic relations have improved immeasurably since the pontificate of the wartime Pius XII. Recent attempts to beatify him have caused renewed anger among Jews, not least in the light of a severely critical biography of him by a Christian author.[16] But the point is that, by and large, Jewish and Roman Catholic officials now trust each other enough to cope with the anger surrounding such inept and even provocative actions. Recent years have not so much diminished the capacity of Jews and Roman Catholics to misunderstand and irritate each other, as they have provided a context of mutual respect that allows discussion and amelioration of fraught issues.

Protestant relations with the Jews have also improved immeasurably.[17] From its beginnings in 1948 until the New Delhi assembly in 1961 the World Council of Churches (WCC) was under the baleful influence of a Barthian theology that regarded religion (often interpreted as non-Christian religions) as unbelief.[18] Since then, this umbrella organization of Protestant and Orthodox churches has issued a number of significant statements. Member churches have also issued their own statements about their church and the Jewish people. The statements by individual churches have had more teeth, since they are binding on their members, whereas the WCC documents have, at best, a moral force only.

I can illustrate the importance of individual churches making their own statements in a personal way. From 1983 to 1995, I was the director of interfaith relations for the British Methodist Church. In 1994, the annual governing body of the Methodist Church passed a resolution about interfaith relations. It included a section that ran as follows:

> A particular relationship which all churches need to get right is that with the Jewish people. Methodists have no special involvement in the shameful Christian history of anti-semitism. Nevertheless, sweeping statements about 'the Pharisees' or 'the Jews' are frequently made from our pulpits as though there were an easy leap from the first century Jews to those at the end of the twentieth century. Recent research has shown the Pharisees in a far more sympathetic light than Christians have hitherto seen them, and this changing perception may mark a watershed in Jewish–Christian relations. The 1940s holocaust largely resulted from, and was justified by, centuries of Christian 'teaching of contempt about Jews'. We, who stand in the shadow of that appalling episode in modern history, cannot perpetuate such attitudes.[19]

It is possible to criticize a number of judgements in that single paragraph and to regret forcefully its evasive second sentence. But the point is that it forbade British Methodists from uttering and acting upon anti-Semitic statements as though they were the continuing teaching of the church. I was accustomed, in that post, to travel in Britain and abroad, talking to church and other groups about Christian relations with people from other religions. I took some pleasure, in the final year of my work, in telling occasional bigots that, not only were their views offensive and dangerous but also they flew in the face of the teaching of the church, so they could not justify such views by reference to an outdated and shameful teaching. Moreover, at the beginning of this chapter, I mentioned the importance of official support for those ordinary people who, in their day-to-day work, see their faith compelling them to engage in good inter-faith relations. The document specifically raises this matter. Its fourth resolution affirms that 'Methodists engaged in working among people of other faiths should be encouraged in their work, and assured of the Methodist Church's warm support for what they do.'[20]

Even so, the British Methodist Church's statement is a minor and ten-tative one. Other churches have been much more forward looking and bold in their positive comments about Jewish–Christian relations. For example, the Evangelical Church of the Rhineland resolved in January 1980 that 'We believe the permanent election of the Jewish people as the people of God and realize that through Jesus Christ the church is taken into the covenant of God with his people.'[21] Coming, as this did, from the heartland of mainland Europe, a place of terror, pain and destruction for the Jews of the Third Reich, this was a remarkably innovative trans-formation of thought and action, offering a new way forward for Jews and Christians to work together.

It takes time for reformed views to be accepted by the rank and file of Christian believers, especially after so many centuries when Jews have been accused of killing the Christ or even murdering God. Still, the effect has been remarkable in transforming attitudes.

It has been met on the Jewish side by a willingness to meet and trust Christians after years when many Jews had felt unable to do either. Perhaps the most interesting recent Jewish document is *Dabru Emet: A Jewish Statement on Christians and Christianity*, put forward as part of the National [US] Jewish Scholars' Project and signed, by more than 170 rabbis and Jewish scholars in November 2000, from the United Kingdom, mainland Europe and Israel, as well as the USA and Canada. (*Dabru Emet* is Hebrew for 'Speak the Truth'.) The Baltimore-based Institute for Christian and Jewish Studies provided the impetus for the document. *Dabru Emet* is an ambitious attempt to present a 'thoughtful Jewish response' to the 'dramatic and unprecedented shift' in Chris-tian–Jewish relations. The opening paragraph reads,

> In recent years, there has been a dramatic and unprecedented shift in Jewish and Christian relations. Throughout the nearly two millennia of Jewish exile, Christians have tended to characterize Judaism as a failed religion or, at best, a religion that prepared the way for, and is completed in, Christianity. In the decades since the Holocaust, however, Christianity has changed dramatically. An increasing number of official Church bodies, both Roman Catholic and Protestant, have made public

statements of their remorse about Christian mistreatment of Jews and Judaism. These statements have declared, furthermore, that Christian teaching and preaching can and must be reformed so that they acknowledge God's enduring covenant with the Jewish people and celebrate the contribution of Judaism to world civilization and to Christian faith itself.

The signatories attest that

> We believe these changes merit a thoughtful Jewish response. Speaking only for ourselves – an interdenominational group of Jewish scholars – we believe it is time for Jews to learn about the efforts of Christians to honor Judaism. We believe it is time for Jews to reflect on what Judaism may now say about Christianity. As a first step, we offer eight brief statements about how Jews and Christians may relate to one another.

These are the eight statements: Jews and Christians worship the same God; Jews and Christians seek authority from the same book – the Bible (what Jews call *Tanakh* and Christians call the 'Old Testament'); Christians can respect the claim of the Jewish people upon the land of Israel; Jews and Christians accept the moral principles of the Torah; Nazism was not a Christian phenomenon; the humanly irreconcilable difference between Jews and Christians will not be settled until God redeems the entire world as promised in scripture; a new relationship between Jews and Christians will not weaken Jewish practice; Jews and Christians must work together for justice and peace.

Not all Jewish scholars who were asked to sign this document felt able to do so, even some sympathetic to closer relations between Jews and Christians. A particular sticking point was about Christian complicity in the Holocaust. It is worth quoting the expansion of this statement in the text:

> Without the long history of Christian anti-Judaism and Christian violence against Jews, Nazi ideology could not have taken hold nor could it have been carried out. Too many Christians participated in, or were sympathetic to, Nazi atrocities against Jews. Other Christians did not protest sufficiently against these atrocities. But Nazism itself was not an inevitable outcome of Christianity. If the Nazi extermination of the Jews had been fully successful, it would have turned its murderous rage more directly to Christians. We recognize with gratitude those Christians who risked or sacrificed their lives to save Jews during the Nazi regime. With that in mind, we encourage the continuation of recent efforts in Christian theology to repudiate unequivocally contempt of Judaism and the Jewish

people. We applaud those Christians who reject this teaching of contempt, and we do not blame them for the sins committed by their ancestors.

Rabbi James Rudin, senior inter-religious adviser of the American Jewish Committee, New York, in refusing to sign the document, wrote that

> Many Christian teachings and actions throughout the centuries prepared the seed bed – the moral, spiritual and intellectual climate – for the rise of genocidal Nazism. Why didn't the statement's Jewish authors address this significant point with the same accuracy and power that many Christians have done? Why is the United Methodist Church's 1996 General Conference declaration on Christian–Jewish relations clearer and stronger about Christianity and the Holocaust than *Dabru Emet*?

It is possible to defend *Dabru Emet* against such a charge, powerful though it is. One line would be to recognize that it is more appropriate and powerful for communities of goodwill to recognize their own short-comings than to have them emphasized by others. Still, I argue below that it is time for a more adult relationship between Jews and Christians, and internal disagreement stemming from a basic benevolence towards the other is to be welcomed as a sign of such growing maturity. However, I shall also argue that it is time that Jews and Christians moved on from emphasizing the Holocaust as the decisive factor in Jewish–Christian relations. It is a moot point whether the signatories to *Dabru Emet* or its dissident voices provide the best way of recognizing the challenge of the Shoah to improved relations, and moving on from it to more centrally important matters.[22] ('Shoah' is a more appropriate word than 'Holocaust' for the extermination of Jews in the Third Reich; it is Hebrew for a great and terrible wind. 'Holocaust' means a burnt offering, and Jews killed under Nazi rule were not offering themselves up as sacrifices.)

This sustained reflection in the form of Jewish and Christian documents on the meaning of Jewish–Christian relations is not paralleled in seriousness and urgency in the wider world of interfaith relations. Many branches of Christianity are set up, even more than Judaism is, with clear, or obvious, structures of authority. This is not matched by many other religions. Even so, there are, in most religious groups, people or institutions that have religious authority. The wider world of dialogue could learn from the recent history of Jewish–Christian relations about the importance of reforming institutional evils that demonize and even seek to destroy the other. It is not enough to leave the resolution of prejudice to people of goodwill. Structures have to change, as well as individuals. Although many religions do not have the equivalent of a pope and curia, most have some form of conferring authority, for example, through the judgements of acknowledged scholars of the religion; and all faiths, even when some of their members claim otherwise, have the capacity to develop beliefs and practices to speak to each new context.

EDUCATION FOR CHANGE

The third question we raised was: what form of education is necessary and acceptable in order to improve Jewish–Christian relations? One area that has been tackled with great bravery and *élan* by post-Shoah Christian and Jewish scholars is that of Christian origins; in particular, there has been a new look at the New Testament. This has been assisted by the official permission of the churches, so that Catholic and Protestant scholars have been encouraged to recover the Jewishness of both Jesus and Paul.

For all the brilliance of many German biblical scholars of the recent past (which has greatly influenced scholars from other countries), the scholarship about Jesus that emerged from their works was often strongly anti-Jewish. They depicted Judaism at the time of Jesus as 'late Judaism' (*Spätjudentum*), as if Jewish religion had ended after 70 CE, or should have. This position was based on the conviction that post-exilic Judaism had ossified and betrayed the prophetic faith of Israel. Jesus stands outside such a hardened, legalistic religion, a stranger to it, condemning the scribes and the Pharisees who were the fathers of Rabbinic Judaism and who have thus misled modern Judaism into perpetuating this sterile, legalistic religion. It is somewhat disquieting that German biblical scholars of the recent past as important, interesting and (in many other ways) perceptive as, for example, Martin Noth, Rudolph Bultmann, Martin Dibelius, Günther Bornkamm and Joachim Jeremias should have depicted Judaism at the time of Jesus in this way.[23] This is particularly so, since most lived through the Holocaust years but still seemed oblivious to the Christian teaching of contempt about Jews, which watered the roots of anti-Semitism, and which persists, even if only as an unconscious and instinctive habit, in their works.

One of the tools by which some Gospel scholars assess the genuineness of a saying or deed of Jesus is the criterion of dissimilarity, which focuses on those words and works of Jesus that cannot be derived from the Judaism of his day (or from the early church). For example, using this criterion, some scholars would claim an authentic word from Jesus when Matthew records his sweeping prohibition of all oaths (5:34, 37; but cf. James 5:12). Yet (among other objections to it), this tool divorces Jesus from the Judaism of his day. He was a Jew, deeply influenced by its unusual emphasis upon belief in one God and God's gift of the Torah to his people. Jesus was not an alien intruder in first-century Palestine. Whatever else he was, he was a reformer of Jewish beliefs, not an indiscriminate faultfinder.

Can we take a step further and admit that anti-Semitism is a feature of the New Testament? The Jewish theologian of the Holocaust, Eliezer Berkowits, disagreed with those who refuse to admit that Christian scripture itself is a cause and the source of the teaching of contempt. In an article entitled 'Facing the Truth', published in the summer 1978 edition of *Judaism*, he wrote that

> Christianity's New Testament has been the most dangerous anti-Semitic tract in history. Its hatred-charged diatribes against the Pharisees and the Jews have poisoned the hearts and minds of millions and millions of Christians for almost two millennia. No matter what the deeper theological meaning of the hate passages against the Jews might be, in the history of the Jewish people the New Testament lends its support to oppression, persecution and mass murder of an intensity and duration that were unparalleled in the entire history of man's degradation. Without Christianity's New Testament, Hitler's *Mein Kampf* could never have been written.

Berkowits challenged Christians about anti-Semitism thus:

> To face this truth is the first condition of meaningful Jewish–Christian dialogue. Is Christianity morally capable of doing it? And what is it able to do about it? (*Judaism*, Summer 1978, p. 323ff.)

The work that persuaded some Christian scholars to face up to the fact that the New Testament itself is seriously flawed in its anti-Semitism was Rosemary Ruether's *Faith and Fratricide*, first published in 1974, before Berkowits's impassioned plea. James Parkes and his successors had argued that anti-Semitism goes back to the church fathers of the second century and later. Ruether, a Roman Catholic theologian, went further and argued that parts of the New Testament were intended to turn Christians against Jews. She described anti-Judaism as 'the left hand of

Christology'. In her opinion, the New Testament's proclamation of Jesus as the Messiah implies the rejection of the Jews, who must suffer for not recognizing him as such. Moreover, the church's beliefs about Jesus led to its self-understanding as the 'New Israel', which renders Judaism obsolete. Ruether enquired, 'Is it possible to say that "Jesus is the Messiah" without, implicitly or explicitly, saying at the same time "and the Jews be damned"?'[24]

This question is sharply put, and we shall return to it later. Certainly, scholarship about Jesus (and also Paul) has been transformed in the last quarter century. We can briefly illustrate this from the works of the Christian Ed Sanders and the Jew Geza Vermes, who were, at one time, colleagues at Oxford University.

Ed Sanders is one of a number of recent scholars who have contributed to the recovery of the Jewishness of Jesus. His great achievement has been to paint the story of Jesus against a wider background of Jewish belief and practice. His *Judaism: Practice and Belief 63BCE–66CE* is an unusual treatment from a New Testament specialist, in that it is a book which is not dominated by Jesus as Christians falsely assume that Jewish faith in that period must have been. In an epilogue to that work, Sanders confesses that

> I rather like the Pharisees. They loved detail and precision. They wanted to get everything just right. I like that. They loved God, they thought that he had blessed them, and they thought that he *wanted* them to get everything just right. I do not doubt that some of them were priggish. This is a common fault of the pious, one that is amply demonstrated in modern criticism of the Pharisees. The Pharisees, we know, intended to be humble before God, and they thought that intention mattered more than outward show. These are worthy ideals.[25]

In *Jesus and Judaism*, Sanders classifies gospel readings under six headings as: certain, highly probable, probable, possible, conceivable and incredible. To give two examples from the extreme points of this spectrum: under 'certain', Jesus certainly proclaimed the kingdom of God to all, including the wicked; under 'incredible', he was not unique in his day in being a Jew who believed in love, mercy, grace, repentance, and the forgiveness of sins, and Judaism was not destroyed as a result of his work. Sanders believes that Jesus offended his Jewish contemporaries in three ways. First, he included the 'wicked', who were outside the law, within the scope of God's kingly rule, even though they remained outside rather than repenting and becoming observant; Sanders believes this inclusion of the wicked in the scope of God's rule to have been a trivial difference. The second offence was the commandment to the prospective disciple to leave his dead father (Matthew 8:21ff.), which conflicted with the law to honour one's parents; this, again, was relatively insignificant, probably a one-off occasion rather than an indication that Jesus intended to oppose, root and branch, the Deuteronomic legislation (Deuteronomy 21:18–21). Third, Jesus' prohibition of divorce (Matthew 9:3–9; Mark 10:2–9) was a radical indication that the Mosaic Law was not strict enough. However, it was the conflict over the temple, which must have struck numerous people as particularly impious, that probably led to his execution. According to Sanders, the threat of destroying and the promise of rebuilding the temple are embedded in the early tradition, and, however interpreted, were, for most Jews, deeply offensive. Yet the Romans executed Jesus, and if Jews had anything to do with it, they must have been those with access to Pilate: the leaders of the priesthood.[26]

Geza Vermes stands in the line of earlier twentieth-century Jewish scholars of Jesus, like Joseph Klausner and Martin Buber, who approved the man's ethical teaching but not the divine status accorded to him by Christians. Vermes's *Jesus the Jew*, first published in 1973, opened the eyes of many to the Jewishness of Jesus, whom Vermes depicted as a Galilean *Hasid*, holy man. He was that kind of Jew rather than a Pharisee, Essene, Zealot or Gnostic. More problematic for Christians was the careful examination of titles claimed for him: prophet, Lord, Messiah, Son of Man, and Son of God. Vermes concluded, controversially, that none of the claims and aspirations of Jesus link him with the Messiah, that no titular use of 'Son of Man' is attested in Jewish literature, and that 'prophet', 'Lord' or even, figuratively, 'Son of God' could be easily applied to holy men in the Judaism of Jesus' day. In works since, Vermes has developed his picture of Jesus. He was a charismatic teacher, healer and prophet.

What then of the Christian church or churches, of the phenomenon of Christianity itself? According to Vermes, the church owes more to the Hellenizing theologies of John and Paul than to Jesus the Jew, to its migration to the Graeco–Roman, gentile world than to its Jewish origins. But Vermes observes that, through the three ancient witnesses of Matthew, Mark and Luke, Jesus the Jew emerges to challenge traditional Christianity of the Pauline–Johannine variety. In Vermes's opinion, the decline in the numbers of Torah-observing Jews who followed the teaching of Jesus without believing the virgin birth or the deification of Christ allowed the dominant Hellenized Christianity a free run. By the beginning of the fifth century, important figures in the church had ruled that it was heretical for Christians of Jewish origin to keep the Mosaic Law. Vermes observes that

> Despite all this, in fairness, it must be emphasized that notwithstanding all its alien dogmatic and ecclesiastical features, Christianity still possesses fundamental elements of the piety of Jesus, such as his emphasis on the purity of intention and generosity of heart, exemplified in a Francis of Assisi who relinquished wealth to serve the poor, and even in our century, an Albert Schweitzer, who abandoned fame to heal the sick in God-forsaken Lambaréné, and a Mother Teresa who, age-old, cares for the dying in the filthy streets of Calcutta.[27]

Much of this thesis is old and somewhat discredited currency and is found in wider circles than those of Jewish–Christian relations. Muslims at the end of the nineteenth century who were anxious to portray their religion as progressive and tolerant did so by drawing on early nineteenth-century biblical scholarship that depicted Paul as the founder of a Christianity that betrayed or at least deviated from the ideals of Jesus of Nazareth.[28] This was not particularly convincing then and has become even less so.

Still, Vermes's representation of the meaning of Jesus is insightful. His work can also be interpreted as a brilliant piece of polemics: he himself converted to Christianity and became a Roman Catholic priest, and then eventually reverted to Judaism.[29] His works are an implicit response to the traditional Christian claim to know what Jewish faith should be and that Jews have got it wrong, in that they insinuate that Jews know what Jesus' faith was like and that Christians have got it wrong. Despite its confrontational nuances, Vermes's work on the Jewishness of Jesus has profoundly influenced Christian writers like his former colleague at Oxford, E.P. Sanders, whose work we have mentioned, and will no doubt long endure. Christians, as well as others who would locate Jesus against his historical background, have reason to be grateful for Vermes's books on Jesus.

This willingness by Christian and Jewish scholars to subject the New Testament to historical criticism to rediscover the past is unusually bold. Such an attitude could profitably though not easily be applied by other faith groups to their scriptures. The treatment of Jesus in the Qur'an does not agree with Christian understanding of what he did and said. Muslims accord the Qur'an the status of God's word, mediated to the Prophet Muhammad through the angel Gabriel. It is therefore difficult for many Muslims to hear Christian criticisms of its accounts about Jesus. A start could be made by more imaginative Muslim commentaries on the meaning of Qur'anic verses, such as that attempted in nineteenth-century India by Sir Sayyid Ahmad Khan (1817–1898). Although, at present, it is hard to see that the willingness of some Christians to evaluate the Bible as a human document would appeal to many Muslims as a model for approaching the Qur'an, some have already begun such a process.[30] Religions have transformed themselves so much in the modern world that it is not beyond the bounds of possibility that Islam and other religions may soon have to reassess certain central beliefs, even though many now believe that such reassessment will never happen.

If education is crucial to transform inter-religious relations in the contemporary world, it is vital that it should be shared as widely as possible. Transformed attitudes about, for example, the New Testament, are not of much use if they remain the preserve of scholars, unknown to churchgoers and synagogue attenders. I have already mentioned the educational work of the Council of Christians and Jews. One further development in the British scene is worth mentioning.

The Times Higher Educational Supplement of 8 December 2000 ran a piece entitled 'A Meeting of Minds Is the Road to Peace'. The subtitle noted that 'as bullets fly over Gaza, academics at Cambridge's Centre for Jewish–Christian Relations (CJCR) are focusing on spreading a message of religious tolerance'. This centre was the brainchild of the Jewish scholar Edward Kessler, who launched it in September 1998. At the time of the article, the centre had fifty students doing an innovative MA in Jewish–Christian relations (the first such MA in the United Kingdom), and two M.Phil. students (one of whom was eighty years old). Fourteen of the MA students were on site and thirty-six studied by distance learning, some from a secure website. There are occasional visiting fellows from a number of countries, and bursaries for students from Eastern Europe and from Israel. Shortly, there will be students funded from the USA. The MA modules are fresh and imaginative. One, for example, examines how Christians and Jews have been perceived in literature and film: caricatures like Shylock and Fagin have often fed the Christian imagination about Jews in negative ways. So this module helps dispel myths and stereotypes.

The centre is located at Wesley House, the Methodist seminary in the Cambridge Theological Federation, within which two hundred students train for various ministries within the Anglican, Roman Catholic, Methodist, United Reformed and Eastern Orthodox Churches. CJCR has a direct input into their training and can thereby hope to inspire future leaders of the churches with new teaching about Jews. CJCR is itself an associate member of the Cambridge Theological Federation. The rather fanciful headline of *The Times Higher Educational Supplement*'s article illustrates why such educational work needs to be done and the crucial importance of such organizations as CJCR to inter-religious dialogue.[31]

A MATURE RELATIONSHIP?

As wicked as anti-Semitism was and remains, is it still an adequate basis for Jewish–Christian relations?

In the post-Holocaust world, it has seemed axiomatic to many Jews and Christians that the Shoah should dominate their discussions. Christians have begun to disentangle the threads of anti-Semitism from the tapestry of their faith and practice. Some Jews have seen Hitler's 'Final Solution' as a defining moment in Jewish history and belief: for example, Emil Fackenheim proposed a 614th commandment to be added to the traditional 613, forbidding Jews to grant Hitler a victory.[32] Yet it is difficult to accept any suggestion that the Holocaust can be compared to Sinai as a seminal revelatory experience. As Jews work out where exactly it does fit into their understanding of God and humanity, both Jews and Christians should ponder whether the Holocaust is of as much moment for their relationship as is the sense of being communities bound in a covenant with each other and with God.

One result of making the Holocaust the centre of Jewish–Christian relations is that it forbids a truly adult relationship, one in which each can respectfully differ from the other. The Holocaust is too bound up with guilt, pain, manipulation and other negative facts to be able to function as the basis for mature reflection. In the past, and even presently in some circles, disagreements have led to anger, alienation and even murder. So it has been natural to seek common ground. The delicate but necessary task for Jews and Christians in the future is to recognize, respect and cope with difference, in the context of respect rather than contempt and animosity. On this point, Jews and Christians might learn from the world of Islam. Although Muslims are often portrayed as unheeding fundamentalists, many are not so. In dialogue with others, they will often present a point of view forcefully and then, with a smile and a shrug of the shoulders say, in Arabic, 'But God knows best.'

Here is one illustration of recognizing difference in the area of biblical studies. The earliest Gospel, that of Mark, calls Jesus 'Messiah' in its first verse. This depiction goes back to Christianity's early moments and may even be part of Jesus' own self-understanding: the Gospel accounts of the entry into Jerusalem seem to confirm this supposition that Jesus believed himself to be the Messiah, even though he gave that concept a particular and peaceable spin (Mark 11:1–11 and parallels). No mainstream Jew believes this. It is much more candid and fruitful for Jews and Christians to recognize this profound difference between them than to avoid the issue altogether or for Christians to play down Christology and its importance to their identity as religious people. On this matter, the views of distinguished Christians like Ruether and Braybrooke are to be resisted. However challenging their views are to Christians, in fact they offer too straightforward a solution to the complexity of the issues involved: they sacrifice the importance of Christian identity for the sake of improved relations. But improved relations cannot be achieved in this way. Most Christians will not be encouraged to improve a poor relationship if the consequence is to deny a central tenet of their faith. A more promising route through the thorny questions is to sort out the tangled threads of Christian theology, to separate 'good' convictions about God from 'bad' ones. Some of the 'good' theology will still be contentious between Jews and Christians. I doubt that Christology is necessarily the left hand of anti-Semitism. It is possible, indeed essential, for Christians to frame a Christology that differs from Jewish beliefs but does not encourage Christians to hate Jews. It is all too easy to fall into the sentimental and unrealistic trap of thinking that fine relations can be built only by agreeing endlessly about things, or else by sweeping differences under the carpet.

Mature Jewish–Christian relationships must surely deal in an honest way with theological issues, not least with disagreements about God. Marcus Braybrooke has noted that, unlike the Council of Christians and Jews, the London Society of Jews and Christians 'has not been constrained to avoid theological discussion'.[33] Nowadays, the LSCJ's position may make better sense in promoting grown-up interaction between Jews and Christians. To some extent, the British CCJ's longstanding doubt about raising theological matters is at odds with the International Council of Christians and Jews (ICCJ). The ICCJ originated in an International Consultative Committee held at Frankfurt in January 1962. In a meeting in Berlin in October 1999, it built on preliminary work to contemplate the involvement of Muslims in an Abrahamic Forum. The British CCJ has been more cautious, so a Three Faiths Forum has recently been founded as an organization to bring together all three monotheistic religions.

This disagreement raises an important issue in contemporary concerns about inter-religious dialogue. Doubtless, there are reasons for continuing bilateral relations between Jews and Christians, as well as extending those associations to other groups. Quite how to resolve this dilemma is difficult to discern, and people of goodwill disagree strongly about it. An important point is that Jewish–Christian relations could benefit from as well as contribute to involvement in the wider world of interfaith dialogue. I offer the example of Israel.

The Council of Christians and Jews has long brought the importance of Israel for Jews to the attention of Christians, although it has been criticized for failing to condemn some of Israel's actions towards its own citizens and neighbours. It has run annual tours to Israel for young adults and for church leaders. Both groups meet Jews and Arabs who present a wide range of different views about Israel; I went on a CCJ tour myself in 1993 and was impressed by the content of the itinerary and its fairness. The subject of Israel raises the issue of Muslim participation in inter-religious debates. For many years, people of the three faiths have been at the forefront of working for peace in their shared holy land.[34] Jews are not the only religious group to locate a particular sacred place as supremely important. The attempt of the Israeli scholar Zvi Werblowsky to argue that Jerusalem is special for Jews in ways that it is not for Christians (who have Rome and the heavenly Jerusalem) and Muslims (who have Mecca and Medina) has interesting points but is not quite free from the charge of special pleading.[35] Still, Jerusalem and Israel are special for Jews in a way that the Vatican is not for Roman Catholics; the importance of Jerusalem and Israel to Jews is more like that of Amritsar and the province of the Punjab for Sikhs. The Punjab, however, is split between largely Hindu India and largely Muslim Pakistan. Since the creation of India and Pakistan in 1947, very few Sikhs have lived in Pakistan, though many important Sikh shrines are to be found there. As a result, some Sikhs have wanted an independent homeland. The sometimes violent struggle for Khalistan has split the Sikh community and caused grave problems in India and countries like the United Kingdom with a significant Sikh diaspora. There would be much to learn from inter-religious ruminations between Jews and Sikhs on the meaning of sacred space. An attempt has already been made to locate the question of Israel within a Jewish–Christian conversation in Asia.[36] Interesting though that is, there is scope for a greater imaginative vision. If the importance of Israel, including the particular issue of Jerusalem, were to be discussed in the context of multilateral religious discussions about other uniquely important sacred spaces, that might prove to be a stimulating and fruitful enterprise.

ORIENTALISM AND OCCIDENTALISM

We need to widen our viewpoint to glance at the relatively recent debate about orientalism and occidentalism. Just as the Holocaust may not be an adequate basis for developing Jewish–Christian relations, one might also say that the wider debate about these academic phenomena is also an insufficient basis for mature inter-religious relationships.

The word 'orientalism' and related terms have been used to criticize Western, often Christian but also Jewish and secular scholars of Islam. These thinkers stand condemned of writing condescendingly about the Orient and of being involved as agents of imperialism to bring about its denigration and devise the destruction of many of its religions and cultures. Abdallah Laroui defined 'orientalist' as 'a foreigner – this case a westerner – who takes Islam as the subject of his research', and continued,

> we find in the Orientalists' work an ideological (in the crudest sense of the word) critique of Islamic culture. The result of great intellectual effort is for the most part valueless The caste of Orientalists constitutes part of the bureaucracy and, for this reason, suffers from limitations that badly inhibit the free creation of new approaches or even the application of those that already exist.[37]

The most scathing critique of orientalism in recent years has been that of Edward Said, by birth a Palestinian Christian, now an American citizen and a secularist. In his influential book *Orientalism* (first published in 1978), he described and condemned the phenomenon in three long chapters: 'The Scope of Orientalism'; 'Orientalist Structures and Restructures' and 'Orientalism Now'. Said's basic point, passionately made, is that 'modern orientalism', from the eighteenth century onwards, has created stereotypes of the gullible, untruthful, illogical, misogynistic, sexually insatiable, cruel and untrustworthy 'oriental' male, and of the passive female. According to Said,

> the principal dogmas of Orientalism exist in their purest form today in studies of the Arabs and Islam. Let us recapitulate them here: one is the absolute and systematic difference between the West, which is rational, developed, humane, superior, and the Orient, which is aberrant, undeveloped, inferior. Another dogma is that abstractions about the Orient, particularly those based on texts representing a 'classical' Oriental civilization, are always preferable to direct evidence drawn from modern Oriental realities. A third dogma is that the Orient is eternal, uniform, and incapable of defining itself; therefore it is assumed that a highly generalized and systematic vocabulary for describing the Orient from a Western standpoint is inevitable and even scientifically 'objective'. A fourth dogma is that the Orient is at bottom something either to be feared (the Yellow peril, the Mongol hordes, the brown dominions) or to be controlled (by pacification, research and development, outright occupation wherever possible).[38]

In short, the proponents of orientalism have argued that Western Christians, Jews and secularists have seen the Eastern religions, particularly Islam but also Hinduism and Buddhism, through the inappropriate and uncomprehending lenses of an all-powerful outsider. Such a well-founded but overstated discourse is understandable in a post-colonial world, but in fact it has generated as much heat as light. 'Occidentalists' are the mirror image of orientalists, in creating a distorted understanding of the West. They have pointed out the grotesque irony revealed in the ways in which non-Western societies have defined themselves in the light of terms and concepts framed by the West.[39] They could as easily have drawn attention to the fact that Muslims and other supposed victims are themselves guilty of failing to figure out the real meaning of the other. There are some sophisticated attempts to blame the West for self-imposed ills in other cultures – for example, the claim that when violence has exploded in the context of Eastern religions it often imitates Western conceptions of collective identity.[40] But most of these endeavours are self-serving. It is true that Western post-imperial political and continuing economic dominance has left gaping wounds upon all concerned, not least the people ruled. But the West cannot forever be held responsible for the shortcomings of others. Most religions teach that all humans are capable of error, if not prone to great sinfulness. At issue is not so much a question of who understands the other, for few seem to

do so on either side of the debate; the real issue is which uncomprehending group or groups have more power to do damage to whom.
There are poignant echoes here of Jewish–Christian relations.

The topic of power is important. It has recently been raised in biblical studies to pose uncomfortable questions. Regina Schwartz, a Jewish
professor of English in Northwestern University, Illinois, has argued that
monotheism has left a violent legacy in history because it defines the
other as being 'not it': so Egypt is 'not Israel'. Diana Eck, a Christian
scholar of Hinduism, has made a similar point:

> In monotheistic consciousness, the singular is the proper number for
> questions of Truth: There is one God, one Only-Begotten Son of the
> Father, one seal of the Prophets, one Holy Book, one Holy and Apostolic
> Church. It might be called 'the myth of monotheism'; that there is one
> and only one holy story to be told, to be reflected upon by theologians,
> and to be participated in by the faithful ... It is a myth in the sense that
> it is the powerful story we tell about reality, so powerful we do not
> recognize it as our story. It is not the world-shaping myth of religious
> people alone, but it is a particular way of seeing and evaluating that has
> shaped equally the world-views of Marxists, secularists and atheists in the
> West.[41]

So opponents to this myth can be seen as in deep error. Schwartz perceptively notes that 'Conquering the Canaanites was a fantasy of an
exiled people; it could only carry force when it was adopted by groups
who held the reins of power in Christendom.'[42] Still, the roots of violence
are present in the Hebrew Bible. The command of Samuel to Saul to
exterminate utterly the Amalekites (1 Samuel 15:3) may have little relevance to a contemporary world without Amalekites, but it locates teaching found in the Hebrew Bible as part of the seedbed from which, with
appalling irony, Christian violence towards Jews grew and flourished. A
generation ago, such an observation would have seemed insensitive and
tactless to many Christians, and loaded with implicit or actual anti-
Semitism to many Jews. A mature relationship should encourage us to
reflect together on hard sayings, not just in the New Testament but also
in the Hebrew Bible, so as to mend the world; we must not bypass them
for the sake of tact or some other secondary virtue.[43] The religion of
Islam shares the same monotheistic tradition. Although medieval Christian depictions of Islam and the Prophet Muhammad were shamefully
biased and libellous,[44] one reason for this was Christendom's sense of
insecurity in the face of Islam's perceived threat to its existence. Islam

made spectacular conquests in its early days, which sorely wounded the Byzantine Empire and threatened the Christian West in a pincer movement from the East and West for many centuries. This debate about monotheism's violent tendencies is one that, if initiated by Jews, Christians and Muslims, could profitably be joined by other voices.

PROSPECTS FOR JEWISH–CHRISTIAN AND WIDER DIALOGUE

Any reflection on Jewish–Christian relations must recognize the enormous strides forward that have taken place since the locust years of Nazi Germany. Thanks to many distinguished scholars and activists, the relationship has been immeasurably transformed for the better. Yet there needs to be a move into a future less dominated by the Holocaust and less obsessed by a need to avoid contentious doctrinal or even missiological issues.

Some apparently forward-looking actions in Jewish–Christian relations may in fact betray a lack of awareness of some of the important issues at stake. Take, for instance, the involvement of Jewish scholars in writing notes for Christian daily Bible readings: in the 2000 edition of the *International Bible Reading Association Notes*, there were three such contributors: Albert Freidlander, Jonathan Gorsky and Jonathan Magonet.[45] They wrote on matters from the Christian Old Testament. Yet this is hardly the 'Old' Testament for Jews, who have no New Testament to supplement it. Christians see in Jesus Christ the fulfilment of the scriptures they share with Jews, whereas Jews locate the latter's meaning in God's continuing dealings with the Jewish people. The Jewish Bible is developed in Midrash and Talmud, and the Christian Bible in church theology. This means that Jews bring very different insights than do Christians to the same work. If the compilers of these daily Bible notes realize this, then the involvement of Jewish contributors might be a splendid attempt to learn from another's world of meaning. If, however, they think that Jewish contributors will merely offer a slightly different point of view to Christian ones, then they have missed the point of what is at stake in dialogue. There are profound differences between Jewish and Christian biblical interpretations, which mirror the two communities' somewhat dissimilar ways of understanding God's presence in the world. This is not to insist that Jewish scholars should not be permitted to write Bible study notes for Christians;

rather, it underlines the necessity that, if this is done, it should be out of a conviction that different and even sometimes incompatible interpretations of God's presence may have much to teach others. We shall turn at the end of Chapter 5 to a discussion of pluralities of truth as part of the post-modern predicament.

The last sixty years have produced much that is worth sharing with those involved in other inter-religious relationships. It remains to be seen whether Jewish–Christian relations might also gain from being mapped on the wider world of interfaith dialogue. If, as we shall explain in the final chapter, John Berthrong and Julius Lipner are on to an important issue in dealing with multiple religious participation and hyphenated religious identity, designations intended to indicate that many individuals are committed to more than one religion, then it would seem unlikely that bilateral relationships, however important and necessary they remain, can exhaust the dialogical imperative of today's pluralist world. So we turn to our final chapter, where we shall explore this matter further in relation to some of the compelling issues that religions must face in the twenty-first century if they are to remain adequate vessels by which Transcendence can grace the world and cause faith to flourish.

5 INTER-RELIGIOUS LIVING IN AN AGE OF GLOBALIZATION

RELIGION IN THE THIRD MILLENNIUM

Conventional wisdom suggests that the power of religion is ebbing away in Western Europe. Although it is certainly the case that institutional Christianity is in deep decline, in other respects conventional wisdom could not be more wrong. This can be illustrated by a glance at a recent work, Rachel Morton's *One Island Many Faiths*, with its subtitle 'The Experience of Religion in Britain'. This book contains seventy photographs of religious Britons and some random comments from them about the importance of their faith. It includes not only representatives of mainstream religions such as Christianity, Judaism, Islam, Hinduism, Sikhism, Buddhism, Jainism, Zoroastrianism, the Bahai Faith and Taoism, but also members of modern reconstructions of faith like Rastafarianism, adherents of indigenous pagan and New Age movements, and those who would describe themselves as non-affiliated seekers after truth.

The human quest for Transcendent reality does not easily ebb away, not even in the face of the flood of scepticism and materialism that has engulfed the West in recent centuries and been exported elsewhere. In my *Religion: A Beginner's Guide*, especially in Chapter 1, I describe how that human quest for something more than meets the eye can be discerned in humankind's earliest history or even prehistory. Although the origins of the human and natural sciences, especially from the mid nineteenth century onwards, were usually avowedly anti-religious, seeking an origin for religion in, for example, sociology and psychology rather than in any genuine revelation from a Transcendent source, this reduction of theology to anthropology has by no means won out as many devoted followers of atheism hoped and believed it would. To be sure, it has wounded mainstream Christian and even Jewish religious observance, but no religion has lasted for ever, a fact that fanatical devotees of one sort of faith or another (including secularists) would do well to keep in mind.

Although the thought that religions fade away and die is a hard one for their adherents to bear, it is demonstrably true in the sense that they flourish, sometimes for centuries and longer, but then die. Transcendence is eternal, whereas human ways of obedience have their moments in the sun, then fade and expire. A case could be made that the longest lasting of all faiths was Ancient Egyptian religion, which flourished from the third millennium BCE and finally petered out in about the fifth century CE.

However, there is another way of looking at the transience of religions. If one moves away from the boundaried definitions of religion so beloved of the Enlightenment West,[1] one can see that contemporary Chinese, Indian, Semitic, primal and other religions, although they have altered and adapted greatly over many centuries and even millennia, have some links with their origins in the dim and distant past in the second millennium BCE, if not earlier. Religions are living organisms, not desiccated relics, so it is entirely understandable that each religion has many and varied forms and interpretations. It is even possible to admit that dead religions cast their shadow upon living ones and may even have shaded, almost imperceptibly, into them. So, for example, modern Hinduism, Buddhism and Jainism are all heirs to the nexus of Indian religion in the first millennium BCE, but they formulated different answers and sometimes even radically different questions to that religious milieu from which they sprang. Once we take clearly the point that religions are not static entities but are affected by culture and even by new and momentous revelatory acts of Transcendent grace, then the variegated expressions of faith in the contemporary world should be seen as natural and explicable in the context of rapid changes.

It is clear that if religions do not renew themselves so that fresh generations of people find them to be transforming institutions, not only will they ebb away, they will deserve to do so as anachronistic and irrelevant phenomena. To be sure, individuals are quite capable of taming and domesticating religions, outwardly embracing them but actually interpreting them in ways that remove their challenge to human self-centredness. This means that not all expressions of religion are authentic. Some are indeed shallow and superficial, reflecting the wish of some of their adherents for fast-food religion. Religion, however, characteristically yields its secrets to those who are deeply committed to it and who work at appropriating its insights. For this reason, some guardians of faith and practice frown upon any change at all as innovative attempts by people to undermine religious authority and power and to sanction their own evil deeds. But this is mistaken disapproval.

The test of true religion is whether it puts people in touch with a Transcendent energy that transforms them and makes their attitudes and actions more just and loving. Does religion truly liberate us, as the Buddha taught? Does it actually help us love God, and our neighbour as ourselves, as Jesus commanded? Does it commend appropriate and energizing relationships in society, as Confucius believed it should? The genius of religions is not that they simply offer good advice about how to live well, but that they also prescribe how this may be done. Moreover, our ability to accept and follow that guidance depends upon our willingness to look beyond shallow and surface phenomena to see deep into the true meaning of life. Theistic religions describe this as a personal God to whose renovating power this world is porous. Buddhism and some other religions reject or ignore the idea of such a being, but are still convinced that the world works in a particular way to which most people have not yet woken up, and that it is necessary to go with the grain of the way the world works if true fulfilment and contentment are to be found.

Accordingly, if religion is to be relevant, it must make sense of the world in which we find ourselves, testing its assumptions but also willing to accept new insights and respond to them in ways that help us to flourish as individuals and in community. This means that religion is not simply the judge of new situations, asking whether they measure up to the standards that religious past precedent has set. Religion has to be humble enough to ask whether our rapidly changing world sets each faith the task of examining its own assumptions to see whether they are meaningful and beneficial for the needs of the third millennium.

So this chapter will now examine the religious possibilities that are open to human beings in an era of globalization. Then it will look at particular issues in the contemporary world that have often been badly handled by religions. We shall discuss three of these (many more could be chosen, but nobody could deny the importance of those discussed here): the role of women; the diversity of human sexuality; and care for the environment. We shall explore these to see if an interfaith and dialogical approach to them might be a more appropriate way to proceed. This leads to the reflection: might such an approach reform and humanize religions, thereby immeasurably improving them? Finally, we shall look at the issues of spirituality and truth in inter-religious dialogue.

BECOMING INTER-RELIGIOUS PEOPLE

In our interconnected world, it is more and more likely that people will live lives that are influenced by more than one religion. It is becoming harder, though it is far from impossible, to live in ghettos. Many people live next to neighbours of another faith. Perhaps their children will marry someone from another religion and so, like it or not, be heirs to more than one way of discerning Transcendence.

Broadly speaking, two particular areas of religious transformation are currently observable in plural societies. The first is the mutual influence that comes from meeting and making friends with people of other faiths. The second is the more unusual yet increasingly common occurrence of what John Berthrong has called 'multiple religious participation'[2] and Julius Lipner has designated 'hyphenated religious identity'.[3] We shall look at both of these in turn, though we shall see that they shade into each other.

I can illustrate the first of these in a personal way. When I first went to India in 1975, as a young man of twenty-three, I had already studied to become a Methodist minister. There I was ordained deacon in the Church of South India, though my ordination to presbyteral orders was scheduled for 1978, after my return to the United Kingdom. In the Methodist ordination service to the presbyterate or priesthood, each candidate for ordination assents to the notion that the holy (Christian) scriptures contain all that is necessary for salvation. Upon my arrival in India, I interpreted that view to mean that Christian faith had nothing to learn from other claimed revelations of Transcendent reality. I think that I was inclined to see negative things about other religions rather than positive things. By the time I was ordained presbyter, I had returned to England and interpreted the words from the ordination service rather differently. By that time, the grace and goodness of so many friends and acquaintances of diverse faiths in India predisposed me to seek what I believed to be the best in another's interpretation of Transcendence. I had also to admit, which I did so freely and gladly after some initial and heart-searching reflection, that they had taught me to look at God in significantly different ways than hitherto. Up till then, I had been influenced by 1960s and 1970s Christian teaching in England that Jesus was your best friend. In India, I learned to modify this rather sentimental and one-sided view, though it is still widely held by some Christians. My Muslim friends taught me much about God as wholly other than humans – a God whose will is to be obeyed and whose nature remains shrouded in mystery though he is the merciful Lord of mercy. My Syrian Orthodox Christian friends from India's state of Kerala taught me that, despite God's utter holiness of being, far removed from sinful humans, we can nevertheless grow into goodness and godliness. To be sure, I could have learned both these insights from my own Methodist branch of Christianity, but I did not. It would be churlish as well as false to maintain otherwise.

So I came to believe that the words at the ordination service that the holy scriptures contain all things necessary for salvation did not mean that Christians (still less, only Methodist Christians) know everything that is to be known about God. I should have learnt that from the apostle Paul when I read how, in sending a letter to the Christians at Corinth, he observed that 'now we see in a mirror dimly, but then face to face' (1 Corinthians 13:11). I now interpret the ordination words to mean that the Christian scriptures witness to and reveal God as God essentially and relationally is to human beings. Christians do not know everything about God. But they know enough to rely upon his grace. So do many people of other religions – if my experiences in India, England and many other places are to make any sense to me.

To believe that God speaks positively and lovingly to other people than those who are members of one's own group does not mean that everybody believes the same thing about Transcendent reality. We do not. Jews and Buddhists do not conceive of Transcendence in the same way. The Muslim belief in one human life and then divine judgement of individuals to heaven or hell is very different from Hindu views of many rebirths of the soul until it is extinguished in Nirvana. There are intra-faith as well as interfaith bickerings and disagreements. The Methodist interfaith theologian and dialogician Kenneth Cracknell has been known to observe that he worships with people of other faith every Sunday in a Methodist church! Later in this chapter, we shall examine the importance of religious truth for and in a religiously diverse world.

Whatever we discover about the importance of truth, surely it cannot deny what we see with the evidence of our own eyes: the holiness of ordinary people of many faiths as they go about their everyday lives. 'Holiness' does not mean an abstract kindliness and goodness. Rather, it means a recognition that this world is porous to Transcendent grace and goodness, which allures us into growing into its likeness. Since, in religiously diverse societies, we are bound (unless we choose to live in geographical or mental ghettos) to come into contact with people of quite different religions than ours yet who strive after holiness, we shall almost certainly be drawn into learning from each other about the ways of Transcendence in her world.

I have already described my own Indian journey into deepening dialogue and understanding. It may be helpful to offer another illustration from my own experience. When my daughter Naomi was born, she came nine years into my married life, much wanted and yet unexpected. Our friends were delighted for us. Hindu friends urged my wife and me to bring her to the local temple. When we did so, a holy woman was visiting from India. She gathered Naomi in her arms and took her into the shrine dedicated to two Hindu deities, where she blessed her and placed the sacred *tilak* on her forehead. It crossed my mind that early missionaries to India like Henry Martyn and William Carey would have regarded this as an appalling and unfaithful act. (There was an amusing irony in that this event took place in a building that had once been the William Carey Memorial Baptist Church.) But this was 1989, not 1789, and, as we have noted, religions grow and develop fresh insights. I was not embarrassed by what happened, and too timid to rescue my daughter. Nor did I decide to put up with what happened for the sake of friendship: I have always believed that what you believe and what you do must go hand in hand. So I was glad and much moved that Naomi was blessed by a representative of another tradition of faith in a Hindu temple. Naomi was born in late December, so I was reminded of the visit of the wise men to the infant Jesus. It pleased me to assume that they were Zoroastrians, Persian scholars of religion who, though they returned home to their books and their learning, knew goodness and holiness and a revelatory act when they saw it; as did I, watching my baby daughter receive her blessing from a representative of a culture and a faith that had, to some extent, nurtured and sustained her father and his faith.

This need to reflect upon and work through why we do what we do in a multi-faith society is crucial to the integrity of those engaged in dialogue. Many Westerners would do well to reflect that, in other parts of the world, people have long had more positive interfaith dialogical relations. In India, for generations Muslims, Hindus, Sikhs and people of other faiths have lived cheek by jowl in friendship and mutual interaction until a recent rise in an exclusive form of Hinduism that closely identifies India with Hinduism and so marginalizes Islam and other faiths. In my edited book, *Ultimate Visions*, in which people reflect on the religion to which they belong, the late Paulos Mar Gregorios, Metropolitan of Delhi and the North in the Malankara Orthodox Church, wrote, 'I went to school [in India's Kerala state] where about a third were Christians, the others following Islam or different varieties of Sanatana Dharma [Hinduism]. As a child I was not brainwashed by Western missionary thinking forcing me to regard and condemn non-Christians as unsaved.'[4] In a similar vein, reflecting on his Christian childhood among Buddhists and Hindus of Sri Lanka, Wesley Ariarajah, who once directed interfaith work for the World Council of Churches, has recorded that he felt 'that it would be unfair on the part of God to receive us, the Christian family, into heaven and send our next-door Hindu neighbours to hell. It was inconceivable to me; it was clearly unfair. I wouldn't want to be in a heaven where our neighbours were not.'[5]

Because of immigration, many people in Western countries now face these issues of squaring an outdated theology with their new circles of friends from diverse faiths, as a matter of urgent practice. Practitioners of dialogue in Britain often come across elderly white people in predominantly Asian areas of town who witness to the quality of their neighbours' faith, and their own. One such person, let us call her Mary, who is typical of many others, will speak warmly of how her Hindu friend Rama takes her shopping or invites her to dinner or to a religious festival that the family is celebrating. She will let slip the comment that she looks after the children while Rama and her husband are at work. Often, she will be puzzled and even dismayed because she has not been taught a theology, a view of God, that matches her experience of others' radiant faith and transparent goodness. Her pastor will tell her that Rama and her family are in deep darkness rather than the light of faith, or else will be unable to resolve the tension between the exclusive and parochial view of God imbibed at theological college and its unsuitability for assessing the holiness of Rama. Admittedly, things are changing. The ignorance of church pastors about other faiths is now more invincible than excusable, since, in recent years, people like me have taught quite another view of God to those being educated as Christian ministers. S...., we need to move on even from that improved situation, in which where we give sympathetic and objective information about other religions, to asking whether it would not make best sense of our experience to tackle the great issues of faith and belief from an interfaith perspective and with the participation of people from other religions.

Mary remains a Christian, but is deeply impressed by Rama's faith and struggles to measure it against the tradition she has hitherto accepted that Christians have all or most of the light of truth. Her inter-religious dialogue has taught her to be sceptical of this tradition, however venerable it is. She may even begin to think that Rama's faith has something in it that her own lacks. Perhaps, she reflects, it is better to believe in many lives leading to the liberation of Nirvana than to believe there is only one existence and then God's judgement, since, if true beliefs lead to good practice, then Hindus certainly seem to look after their old people better than many Christians do. What Mary needs is a theology, a belief about Transcendent reality, that enables her to respect the convictions of other people yet also helps her to choose what she can learn from them but also what she can, and maybe even must, disagree with. Through this process of inter-religious dialogue, Mary is on the move towards a way of believing and living her faith that is more appropriate – truer about God, herself and her neighbour – than the one she had.

There are many people like Mary, not just in the Christian religion and in Western culture. I have listened to people of many faiths explain to me how an austere, exclusive and condemnatory interpretation of their religion's attitude towards outsiders no longer makes any sense to them, even though they continue to cherish that religion. I was much moved when a Muslim friend told me that he had dreamed that he was dying and I was there to say prayers for him as he passed from this world to the next. Friendship enables and spurs us to talk openly about things that matter to us, including religion; it makes us see unexpected links and disagreements and encourages us to cope with working at what they mean.

The stories of my daughter and of Mary and Rama have moved us, almost imperceptibly, from the first area of mutual religious influence to that of hyphenated religious identity and multiple religious participation. Let us try to explore the area where the one area shades into another.

The urgency to puzzle through where Transcendence is to be found in the midst of religious diversity is an issue for all faithful people, but is particularly acute for some. Nowadays, more people than ever marry outside their religion. Most religions have frowned upon this, and some have not allowed it. Islam forbids Muslim women to marry non-Muslim men, but is nevertheless powerless to stop it happening in many places. Judaism, in its Orthodox form, determines who is a Jew through the mother's line, so, if a Jewish man marries outside his religion, his children cannot be regarded as Orthodox Jews, unless their mother converts before the birth of the children. One result of religious authorities insisting on maintaining traditional beliefs is that such inter-religious families, who may want to be identified with religious belief and practice, feel let down and alienated. Very rarely are such religious authorities asked to justify their actions. Many people assume they are simply being faithful to their faith's fundamental meaning. Yet there are good reasons to doubt this. All religions grow and develop over time. The history of religions allows us sometimes to take a sceptical view of religious leaders, who often, no doubt unintentionally for the most part, miss the wood for the trees. We may recollect the Buddha's critique of certain Hindu leaders of his day, or Jesus' condemnation of religious men who interpreted faith in ways that laid burdens on others' backs.

When such exponents tell us that God forbids certain things, that permits us to deduce certain things about their portrayal of God. Is it a worthy or credible interpretation of God in the third millennium CE to maintain that God disapproves of interfaith or multicultural marriage?

When people who live and love in religiously diverse societies do what they feel they must, irrespective of backward-looking religious grandees, then they are drawn into a new kind of faithful living. An Indian Christian friend of mine, almost my sister, is married to a Hindu. They recently bought land to farm. They then participated in a Hindu rite to bless and sanctify the new enterprise upon which they were engaged. At about the same time, after years of lacking much formal contact with a church, my friend formally joined a nearby church. She provides an example of multiple religious participation: she belongs, in some sense, to more than one religion. Of course, she has done so for many years. People like her face these issues in relation to such matters as how to bring up children. Since religions, though they change and adapt, are essentially conservative, not only in negative ways but in the positive sense that they conserve and pass on tried and tested patterns of faith and practice, it is not easy for people to break the mould and set out on courses that have rarely been explored before and that have been regarded with suspicion if not outright hostility. But nowadays more people than ever are attempting to interpret their faith in the light of the choices they have made in a plural society that have hitherto been condemned or hardly ever tried and tested.

John Berthrong has pointed out, in his wise, witty and entertaining work, *The Divine Deli*, that to a great extent 'MRP-ing', as he calls people's involvement in more than one religion, is a fact of life in North America. (He addresses specific situations there, but would agree that MRP-ing is increasingly visible in Europe and other areas where it has hardly ever existed before.) People borrow from variant readings of truth, they get caught up in matters of marriage, meditation and the environment and blend together different views from a variety of religions to locate and live out their convictions. To be sure, MRP-ing may be little more than cocktail religion for the chattering classes, for whom idle conversation is a substitute for deep commitment. That may very well be the future of religion for many people in the contemporary Western world. Still, it would be unfair to accuse all MRP-ers of that. One may criticize the gullibility of many young people who, mainly in the 1960s and 1970s but also today, have sought light from the East to clarify the meaning of their materialistic lives, and who often found conmen and conwomen who brewed a potent blend of sex, money, yoga and drugs and relieved them of their money. Gita Mehta's hilarious exposé, *Karma Cola: Marketing the Mystic East*, is an unputdownable read. Still, the sincerity of most of these young people and their unwillingness to accept stale and irrelevant faith can hardly be denied.

MRP-ing has been a fact of life in some parts of the world for millennia, not least in China and Japan. In Nigeria, my wife's native country, not only do Christians, Muslims and practitioners of African traditional religion live cheek by jowl; often the same family will have representatives of each of these faiths and think nothing much of it. (This is, problematically, changing, in the face of more fundamentalist interpretations of Islam, a resurgence of self-confident traditional religion, and post-colonial Christian self-absorption.) When I was a pastor in London, I was occasionally asked to bless the marriage of Japanese couples, who mostly did not speak English and were on their honeymoon. They felt, although they were Shintoists, that it was appropriate for a wedding to be conducted in a Christian church and that the bride should wear white. This is an updated variation on a traditional East Asian theme that people engage with different religious practices for different rites of passage, at birth, marriage and death, and yet these various customs are refracted through a particular, overriding commitment. So, in Japan, a couple may be Shinto but still want a Christian blessing on their marriage, and in China a man may be essentially a Confucianist in his allegiance yet participate in Buddhist and Taoist rites at various times in his life. Even if it is the case that one religion provides the focus of MRP-ing, Berthrong writes that 'it is not uncommon for East Asians to claim that they participate faithfully in more than one tradition even if this seems impossible from a Western perspective'.[6] He goes on to ask in what senses he can regard himself as a Confucian-Christian, given his life experience.

So we encounter hyphenated religious identity. We have seen that some people, by virtue of their marriage, the customs of their ancestors, or for some other reason, engage for much of their lives with more than one expression of religious identity. Others take this a step further: by reason of deep personal commitment, they are devoted to more than one religion. As I have already mentioned, a close friend of mine calls himself a Parsee-Christian. Brought up as a Parsee, he became attached to Christian faith as a young man. Yet the memory of his loving Parsee grandmother, whose affection and tenderness arose from her strong faith, still remains with him many years later. He has no wish to describe his religious journey as a movement from darkness to light. Somehow he has to hold both religions in tension to make sense of who he is and what he is becoming.[7]

In much of this book and especially in Chapter 3, I have argued that dialogue must be done interfaith and that such dialogue is essential to discern what Transcendence is like and how it regards us. The great and prophetic voice in this area has been that of Wilfred Cantwell Smith, the Canadian historian and theologian of religion, who died in 2000. He argued that, if Christians affirm that theirs is a monotheistic faith in one creator, God, there can be no parochial Christian theology. It makes no sense at all for believers in one God to talk of 'my God' and 'your God'. Theology must therefore be done dialogically and interfaith so as to understand the divine reality that most Christians confess as Trinity but others differently affirm. To explore this insight was the purpose of Smith's remarkable book, *Towards a World Theology: Faith and the Comparative Study of Religion* (1981), which can be seen as the natural development of his concerns over forty years of academic and humane work. Smith believed that such a global theology was what great Christian figures like Aquinas, Calvin and Luther believed they were exploring. They were interested in articulating a universal theology, not a sectarian one.[8] In our contemporary context, how can we embark on such an enterprise without reaching across boundaries and exploring with others? The scale of that endeavour may be greater, but it is not entirely new. The great medieval theologian, Thomas Aquinas, was deeply indebted to translations of Arab and Greek works by Muslim authors, and we have noted in Chapter 2 that Wesley was persuaded of the case for a universal theology not least because of his conviction that faith and works are fruitfully and mutually related in godly living and godly dying.

If there is truly a need for a universal theology, we must be willing to join with a number of other voices in articulating it. And if it is truly universal, it must address and mend areas of darkness where religions have usually stumbled and fallen short in their understanding of the will of Transcendent grace. So we move to three such subjects: the role of women, the diversity of human sexuality, and care for the environment. Our discussion should cause us to reflect: would not an inter-religious and dialogical discussion liberate the religions from outmoded views and help mend the world?

THE CHANGING ROLE OF WOMEN

The women's movement began before the modern interfaith movement, whose origins can be traced to the First World Parliament of Religions held during the Columbian Exposition in Chicago in 1893. The women's movement began rather earlier that century. Indeed, one of the nineteen women plenary speakers in Chicago was Antoinette Brown Blackwood, who was the first Christian woman to be ordained. That event took place on 15 September 1853, in the Congregational Church, when Blackwood became pastor of the South Butler congregation in New York State for a short time.[9] She emphasized the need for more women to be active as preachers and speakers, for she saw the work of women as 'indispensable to the religious evolution of the human race'.[10] Blackwell wrote to her friend, Lucy Stone, of the Parliament of Religions, that it 'was a grand demonstration in favor of toleration and an underlying unity for all. It was like a new Pentecost.'[11]

In Judaism, women became rabbis somewhat later. The first woman rabbi in Britain was ordained in 1976. Earlier in the century, Regina Jonas (1902–1944) was ordained a rabbi in Germany, causing a scandal;

she died in the Auschwitz concentration camp.[12] In some South Asian religious experience, a different tale can be told of women's importance as religious leaders. In due course, we shall enquire how it may be heard by others in dialogue.

To liberal-minded people, it seems extraordinary that only in the nineteenth century CE or sometimes even later were issues of fundamental rights for women raised and were women allowed a say in their own vocations and fulfilment. Not just in Christianity but also in some other faiths, it was recognized by at least some men as well as many women that religions were patriarchal and oppressive to women. The Indian Muslim biographer of the Prophet Muhammad, Syed Ameer Ali (1849–1928), wrote that the spirit of the Prophet's laws would lead to the emancipation of women. But he did not understand the problematic nature of such a claim, just as many Christians miss an important point when they emphasize Jesus' remarkably relaxed and inclusive attitude towards women. There is just the faintest whiff of condescension about such claims, as though women should be grateful for the crumbs that fall from the table of equality. Ameer Ali, broad minded though he was compared with others of his day, gave his own position away when, in an article of 1899, he asserted that 'women have and always will be, what men make them', and claimed that 'the idealization of womanhood is common to all creeds and nations who have made any advance in civilization. The highest natures crave for an exemplar in whom they can find embodied, or whom they can invest with, all that is pure and divine in women.'[13] An implication is that the possessors of 'highest natures' are men, not women.

Sometimes religious men find a particular woman exemplar to embody their fantasies about what women should be and do. One example of this are the domestic duties and also the somewhat unedifying and abusive sexual role assigned by many men (and, alas, by some women) to the Virgin Mary.[14] Understandably, feminist writers have strong criticisms to make of the way in which men manipulate, consciously or otherwise, important female religious figures to justify and impose patriarchal attitudes on women as the will and delight of Transcendent reality, and fool and delude themselves that this gives Transcendental sanction to bigotry. Such inappropriate assumptions still motivate even men of goodwill. In discussing the global ethics project in Chapter 2, I noted the strange assumptions behind its third directive: 'Commitment to a culture of equal rights and partnership between men and women.' Ursula King has posed the problem succinctly and devastatingly: 'The directive is phrased as if the religions already had the answer to the oppression and exploitation of women, whereas religions themselves are part of the problem and cause of this oppressive state of affairs.'[15]

This raises the issue of whether Transcendent reality is incorrigibly and inherently patriarchal and sexist, predisposed to favouring men over women, so that religions merely reflect and embody the will and being of supra-mundane truth. Many religious people defend sexist and chauvinist beliefs and practices as if God, however named, was similarly prejudiced, and even a man. In the British Methodist Church's recently revised liturgical book, one act of Eucharistic worship cautiously calls upon God as 'our Father and our Mother'.[16] Howls of protest arose, though it should be noted that the book was duly authorized for use in Methodist churches in the annual governing body of the church, by a large majority vote. According to classical Christian doctrine, God is 'without body, parts and passions'. It seems obvious that God cannot be designated as male by virtue of 'his' chromosomes or genital arrangements, though many people still fail to come to terms with this plain fact. Most world cultures have been and still are patriarchal, so it is natural that largely male imagery should be used to describe divine reality, but religions are usually careful to specify that Transcendent participation in human reality is either beyond gender or else to be intuited in both genders. Religions like Islam and Buddhism characteristically regard Transcendence as beyond male and female distinctions.[17] In Hinduism, an avatar of God can be in male or female form; sometimes, at a popular level, eunuchs or people who possess features of both genders, are seen as channels of divine reality. In Christianity, which claims that God became incarnate as a male human being, theologians have usually been careful to argue that he became human and participated in our common humanity.

Much of this book has argued for or implied the need for religions to be relevant. If they are not, they will perish like the dinosaurs, and deserve to. The reactionary argument that such change is godless innovation fails to recognize that all religions grow and develop in time, surviving by virtue of making sense of their past wisdom for present circumstances. To be sure, religions are conservative, conserving tested and tried insights about and from Transcendent reality. But sometimes they preserve bad practice. Few people would now justify the practice of slavery on religious grounds, though until comparatively recently it has been warranted by Christians among others. Slavery was not abolished in the British Empire until 1833, and not in China until 1910. The appalling and dehumanizing shadow that slavery cast across the mindset of societies who practised it lingered on for a long time. Indeed, the Englishman James Hunt (1833–1869), president of the newly formed Anthropological Society, declared in 1863,

> that the Negro is a different species from the European; that the analogies are far more numerous between the Negro and the ape than between the European and the ape; that the Negro is inferior intellectually to the European; that the Negro can only be humanized and civilized by Europeans.[18]

These words were uttered during the American Civil War (1861–1865), which was fought to a great extent over the issue of black slavery. Hunt's words are a reminder that the secular disciplines were not value-free, 'scientific' pursuits, but were used to justify practices like enslavement and imperial subjugation by a 'master race'; practices that are now rightly condemned. Secular disciplines can be just as imperious and domineering in their claims as religion; and just as destructive, if not more so. But this hardly gets religions off the hook.

In their early periods, most religions rarely saw the harm in slavery. In Christianity, for example, although it can be claimed that Jesus said nothing about slavery as an institution and that Paul urged the kindly treatment of slaves by their masters, slavery was still accepted. Paul's charming letter to Philemon returns the (possibly runaway) slave Onesimus to him, urging his acceptance back into Philemon's household as a useful (a pun on Onesimus) member. In the early centuries of Christian history, only Gregory of Nyssa saw the point that slavery was contrary to the logic of Christian teaching.[19] Islam and many other religions similarly took a long time to get the point that Transcendent grace and goodness does not require the humiliation and subjugation of some of her children by others. The classical world of Greece and Rome was run on slavery, for all its religious, philosophical and other achievements.

Although some men and even women are content to accept patriarchal religious belief and practice, these are unacceptable not only on humane grounds but because they malign the character of Ultimate Reality. If Transcendence really encourages slavery, that makes liberal-minded humans better than God in their commitment to such values as justice and love, which are traditionally sourced from supra-mundane truth. Similarly, it makes a mockery of our deepest views about God for men to define and oppress women on the basis of an imputed divine sanction. In a hundred years' time, one hopes people will see patriarchy as as misguided an ethos as most religious people now view slavery, and will wonder why it could ever have been justified by appeal to religious precedent.

Such necessary transformations as the abolition of slavery and gender inequality are hard for religions (and also secular ideologies) to deal with, because they require neither the view that all things are the best in the best of all possible worlds, nor a utopian belief that things can and will only get better. What is needed is an intelligent rather than naïve commitment to progress and development. The nineteenth century had a rose-tinted attitude towards (mainly secular, but to some extent religious) progress, which was disillusioned by the two world wars of the following century. But that does not undermine theories of development in our understanding of religious truth; rather, it requires us to test them. The test is one of transformation: does progress make us more obedient to and even like Ultimate Reality as we construe it? We shall return to this point, and contend that such a construal can be forged in the furnace of inter-religious dialogue.

Lots of thinking religious people are aware of the importance of the women's movement in Christianity and perhaps Judaism, but not in Islam. Many Westerners fear Islam and so can hardly believe that the women's movement is now a significant issue there. It is, so let us examine aspects of the women's movement in contemporary Islam and reflect on its meaning for religions in our diverse world. We have seen the tentative and patronizing, yet certainly well-intentioned and not bogus, recognition by Ameer Ali that much treatment of women within the Islam of his day would not do. Other nineteenth- and twentieth-century Muslim modernizers in Egypt, India and elsewhere made similar and often equally condescending observations. When I worked in India in the 1970s, there were many little books available by Muslim men on the role of women, justifying the Prophet Muhammad's marriages, lauding the revelatory laws of inheritance he brought for women, and so forth. Most of these could be condemned on a number of grounds, not least that of unpersuasively presenting a theoretical ideal with actual practice. For example, it may indeed be the case that God, through the Prophet Muhammad, prescribed generous inheritance laws for women but that begs the question of whether such laws are actually followed in specific societal contexts or are simply ignored or applied in ways that annul their generosity? Furthermore, despite the popular Muslim belief that the generous inheritance laws for women were a first in world history, this is not true. Such laws were not new to Roman, Sassanian and other older cultural practices.[20]

More recently, Islamic feminists such as Leila Ahmed[21] and Fatima Mernissi have brought a sharper focus and greater measure of authenticity to the wider Muslim debate about gender issues. It is instructive to consider Mernissi's life and feminist perspective. A Moroccan sociologist born in 1940, she was brought up in a harem, and describes her childhood in her wonderfully evocative and sympathetic book *The Harem Within*. No wonder, therefore, that some of her most exciting work has been to explore the image of the veil as a feature of traditional male–female roles in Islam. If the Virgin Mary's importance in much of Christianity has resulted in certain views of women as chaste and asexual because of their supposed biological inferiority to men, then, in Mernissi's view, Islam's take on sexuality has been rather different. Male Muslim thinkers from the early days regarded women's sexuality as a threat to civilized society and elaborated rules to control it, which can be symbolized in the veiling of women. This protects the women, and indeed men and society as a whole, from female potency. Still, Mernissi contends that

> The existing inequality [in Islam] does not rest on an ideological or biological theory of women's inferiority, but is the outcome of specific social institutions designed to restrain her power: namely, segregation and legal subordination in the family structure. Nor have these institutions generated a systematic and convincing ideology of women's inferiority. Indeed, it was not difficult for the male initiated and male-led feminist movement to affirm the need for women's emancipation, since traditional Islam recognizes equality of opportunity.[22]

This is a problematic statement. Was the feminist movement in Islam really led by men and, if it was, should it have been? Can one group unilaterally initiate or control movements for true equality or complementarity, or must such actions not be dialogical? Although the case is sometimes made by Muslims that Islamic feminism is based on different principles from Christian or secular feminism and is a separate movement, is this not special pleading? It looks as though some Muslim women have been influenced and inspired by Christian feminist movements to look again at the roots of Islamic teaching and reinterpret them in more inclusive ways.

Would it not be more generous and accurate for Mernissi to argue for her own and other Muslim women's indebtedness to Christian women's work as an impetus for their own, however different the conclusions of both groups might be? Mernissi's analysis of Christian attitudes to female sexuality contains faint echoes of the attitude that has bedevilled much Christian writing about Islam in the last two centuries, and *vice versa*: comparing the idealistic best in your own religion with a negative, stereotypical and sometimes insufficiently informed appraisal of the other's.

Mernissi's thesis presupposes that present Muslim practice belies both its future potential and also the actual customs of its past golden age. That long-ago period is usually presented as the Prophet Muhammad's lifetime and the reigns of the first four 'rightly guided' caliphs. Let us explore aspects of Mernissi's treatment of this period. It will be instructive to compare her with Ameer Ali, whose views about women have already been introduced; he is one of the Muslim men whose work contributed to what Mernissi calls the 'male initiated and male-led feminist movement'.

Many Muslim modernists like Ameer Ali, responding to Christian and other criticisms about aspects of the Prophet's teaching about customs that involve women, have attempted to interpret Muhammad's practice in the light of the times and place he lived. Muslim modernizers have often done this in broad brushstrokes. So, for example, Ameer Ali wrote that

> With the progress of thought, with the ever-changing conditions of this world, the necessity for polygamy disappears, and its practice is tacitly abandoned or expressly forbidden. And hence it is, that in those Moslem countries where the circumstances which made its existence at first necessary are disappearing, plurality of wives has come to be regarded as an evil, and as an institution opposed to the teachings of the Prophet; while in those countries where the conditions of society are different, where the means which, in advanced communities, enable women to help themselves are absent or wanting, polygamy must necessarily continue to exist.[23]

Ameer Ali's argument is that Muhammad's situation was very different from that in modern times, so the Prophet's prescriptions need no longer bind all Muslim women. Further, circumstances will progressively change to bring about the end of polygamy. Most Muslims believe that certain Qur'anic verses had their force abrogated during the lifetime of the Prophet, because new situations called forth new duties. Moreover, the collections of Hadith (traditions about what the Prophet said and did, taken from evidence of his earliest and closest followers) pay close attention to the importance of the date and context of Qur'anic revelations and prophetic words and deeds, and do not simply commend them as acontextual rules for sound belief and behaviour. Nevertheless, many Muslims act as though the Prophet were a supra-historical person whose words and deeds can easily be applied to any time and place (just as some Christians treat Jesus in a like fashion). The question remains: can they? If not, then such Muslims may need to amplify how the Prophet's life remains exemplary for Muslims and all who would strive to obey God's word in the contemporary world.

Fatima Mernissi provides a more subtle way of emphasizing the contextual importance of Prophetic action and Qur'anic revelation. For example, she claims that the *hijab* verse (Qur'an 24:31), commanding the Prophet's wives to speak to men from behind a veil, came for these women's protection. She depicts the Prophet as reluctantly forced by the misogynistic Umar (later the second caliph) to compromise his principles for the pragmatic value of providing security for his wives in the volatile aftermath of the siege of Madina by the Quraysh, his Makkan opponents from whose ranks Muhammad sprang.[24] That expediency should have been temporary. What really matters is that Muhammad, unlike many contemporary Muslims 'acknowledged the importance of affection and sex in life. And, during expeditions, his wives were not just background figures, but shared with him his strategic concerns.'[25]

The implication is clear: Muslim men should follow the intention of Muhammad to engage with women as honoured companions. Mernissi and other Muslim feminists perform a valuable though controversial service in reminding their co-religionists that the Qur'anic and Hadith texts may have different and more limited implications than are found in the pious assumptions and acts of many Muslim men.

Conservative Muslims argue that such judgements are misguided and often malevolent. They tend to believe that many contemporary feminist expectations, whether of Muslims or other women, are contrary to the word of God, and that their implementation must be resisted. Many Muslim feminists recognize that Western women's concerns are not necessarily those appropriate to Muslim women, who must find their own path to a liberating future. What that path is seems less clear. Understandably, many Muslim women are keen to avoid antagonizing conservative Muslim opinion, so their private beliefs do not always gain a public airing. Clearly, discussion in this area has moved on since Ameer Ali's day.

Even so, here again is an issue involving the authority of the original sacred documents. Mernissi is relatively comfortable questioning the authority of some of the Hadith. She portrays Aisha, the Prophet's favourite wife, as a faithful interpreter of authentic traditions about her husband and as a scourge of those who transmitted false Hadith. For example, Aisha noted of Abu Hurayra (died *c.* 678), who is said to have narrated an immense number of Hadith, including many disdainful of women, that 'He is not a good listener, and when he is asked a question he gives wrong answers.' On one occasion, she refuted one of his Hadith which ran, 'Three things bring bad luck: house, woman, and horse.' Aisha explained that

> He came into our house when the Prophet was in the middle of a sentence. He only heard the end of it. What the Prophet said was: 'May Allah refute the Jews; they say three things bring bad luck: house, woman, and horse.'

Not surprisingly, Aisha and Abu Hurayra did not get on, as this account illustrates:

> When she said to him, 'Abu Hurayra, you relate Hadith that you never heard,' he replied sharply, 'O Mother, all I did was collect Hadith, while you were too busy with kohl [a kind of eye-shadow] and your mirror.'

Although Abu Hurayra is remembered as a pious man, and the most revered collections of the Hadith incorporate some of his material, Aisha may have had a point. The Caliph Umar, a notable misogynist, is supposed to have said, in relation to remembering Hadith, 'We have many things to say, but we are afraid to say them, and that man there [Abu Hurayra] has no restraint.'[26]

Ameer Ali was extremely critical of Aisha. Like many Shia Muslims, he believed her to have played an active role in seeking to bring down, unjustly in his view, the Caliph Ali, whom Shia Muslims revere and believe should have succeeded the Prophet as his immediate political and spiritual heir.[27] Ameer Ali displayed no interest in the Sunni interpretation of Aisha as a gatherer and preserver of many important Hadith. Unlike Mernissi, he hardly mentions the Hadith at all; still less does he subject them to any serious historical criticism.

Ameer Ali associated the Qur'an with the mind of Muhammad;

whereas Mernissi, more cautiously, denies the authenticity of certain Hadith. However, both raise, she more by implication than directly, the question of how revelation is revelatory. Many Muslims would challenge Mernissi's view of the Hadith, on the grounds that they are a secondary form of revelation, guaranteeing the Prophet's role as guardian of the *umma* by accurately recording words and deeds associated with him. They are seen as sacrosanct, immune from human criticism. More troubling to many Muslims is the insinuation, from Mernissi's accounts of the Prophet's life, that the Qur'an is involved in the human and the provisional. For example, the *hijab* verse is Qur'anic. On Mernissi's reading of that verse's context, did God or the Prophet permit it reluctantly and pragmatically? If so, how is the Qur'an revelatory? There are serious issues here of Qur'anic authorship and immutability that Mernissi does not unpack. Her modernist questionings take her so far, but imply more than they deliver.

Perhaps the issues could be seen better from a different perspective. Instead of looking to the past primarily for good practice to improve the present and provide hope for the future, maybe Ameer Ali had a point (however poorly made and illustrated) when he saw the necessity for principles of growth, development and progress. In other words, the earliest period of any religion is not the place where we should look for an idealized society. Rather, it provides the seedbed for ideals, new possibilities and visions that can galvanize succeeding generations into implementing transforming ways of life. It is understandably true that religions are reluctant to criticize their heroes and earliest times: for example, Christians commonly praise Jesus for his open-ended attitude to women but often offer no plausible reasons why no woman was included among the twelve disciples. Similarly, Buddhists extol the Buddha's fair-minded treatment of women but often fail to deal with the deeper implications of the story that at first he refused ordination to women, and was persuaded otherwise only by his aunt and stepmother, Queen Mahapajapati, who, with a group of five hundred women, sought ordination from him.[28] A large part of the allure of the foundational figures in each religion is that they can see possibilities hidden from their followers, whom, nevertheless, they can inspire to deeper insights and transformed lives. Still, even the greatest heroes remain located within their own world. Another aspect of these figures' attractiveness is their openness to be transformed themselves by the logic of their own teaching. We have already noted the Buddha's willingness to accept the request of his aunt for ordination; the penny dropped for him that his own teaching demanded that he grant her appeal. Another example is Jesus' eventual willingness to heal a foreign woman because of her great faith, even though his initial words to her seem to show that he shared the common human suspicion of the other (Mark 7:24–30).

Dialogue between friends of different faiths often raises questions of the constraints upon people like Jesus, Muhammad and the Buddha. Although authoritative leaders in each religion often surround them with the odour of sanctity and discourage people from asking searching questions, individuals still do often manage both to revere their iconic figures yet also to recognize that they were bound by the horizons of the knowledge and culture of their time, as are all people.

Some feminist writers have argued that it is relatively unimportant whether women are ordained to the priesthood, the rabbinate or some other authoritative position. In their view, much more profound structural changes are needed in order to transform the expectations and dynamics of the religions. One can agree with the need for such a revolution without underplaying the importance of seeing women in traditionally respected positions. For example, when I went to theological college in 1973 to train for Methodist ministry, there were women there for the first time. The annual governing body of the church had agreed that women could be ordained. Many men in the college, and even male members of staff, expressed reservations about this innovation. Women have not had a smooth ride since, but remarkable changes have taken place in the minds of Methodist worshippers. There are many stories of members of Christian congregations refusing to contemplate having a woman minister, yet changing their minds within weeks of her arrival. So it is important not to disparage the influence of women in positions of religious power.

In the world of inter-religious dialogue, women are still conspicuous by their absence. Although they are present at formal dialogical meetings, they are often excluded from photographs taken of the very eminent people there. Rarely are feminist positions aired, still less taken seriously. Many men seem to think that if a handful of women are invited, they should be grateful and non-confrontational. So it is with good reason that Ursula King has written that 'it is evident that inter-religious dialogue remains part of patriarchy'.[29]

There are two serious problems with this absence of specific women's voices in formal inter-religious dialogue. The first is that, without them, men cannot hope to be radically transformed by new possibilities of mutual learning. The second is that women themselves can remain in ignorance of certain important issues and thus themselves pass on either uninformed prejudices or else a partial reading of religion as its true meaning.

Although the feminist movement in Christianity has frightened many defensive men, a growing number of books by men shows that it has led to their transformation, too, as well as the liberation of women.[30] Men no longer have to defend and embody macho attitudes; they do not need to shun tenderness and tears, they can connect with their intuitive selves. This may seem to imply rather a narrow, conventional and even prejudiced view of what constitutes masculinity and femininity. The growing involvement of men in women's issues, not as self-appointed independent and final arbiters of what constitutes women's nature and rights, but as partners in exploring what it means to be truly and fully human, is bound to start in tentative and rather gauche ways but will hopefully blossom into fruitful and transformative dialogue.

The earliest phases of feminist theology in its Christian and post-Christian forms often resulted in depreciatory remarks about the patriarchal God of the Old and New Testaments. Although Mary Daly's ammunition is directed against Christianity, she states that 'the history of antifeminism in the Judeo-Christian heritage already has been exposed. The infamous passages of the Old and New Testament are well known.'[31] She points also to atrocities against women in Indian, Chinese, African, European and American religions. Religions have justified or at least condoned widow burning, foot binding, genital mutilation, witch burning and other such appalling phenomena.[32] Whatever the (no doubt justifiable) pain and anger in Daly's works, and in those of similar feminist theologians like Daphne Hampson, their alienation from most religious traditions seems to leave them at the disadvantage of speaking only to themselves and their acolytes.

Surely it would be better if more women were involved in interreligious dialogue. Then maybe more men would see the points they are making. Maybe women would also then listen to a greater diversity of opinions than at present many of them do. Daly's picture of religious malpractice can be faulted not so much for what it records of religions' defects as for what it fails to make of their transforming virtues, even for women who were marginalized and even tortured and killed, many of whom saw other meanings within the systems that oppressed them. Whatever criticisms can be made of the work of Fatima Mernissi, discussed earlier in this chapter, she stands as an example of someone who sees more positive and transforming possibilities in her religion. In her view, many of these possibilities have been suppressed by men but could be reclaimed or else seen as more positive and appropriate contemporary developments of Islam.

It is possible and even likely that, throughout this section, I have misunderstood or only partially comprehended women's issues in the contemporary inter-religious world. However regrettable this is, it simply underlines the point that dialogue is the only certain way to a more acceptable and well-informed stance. When men alone talk about women and religion, without any intention to involve women as full and equal partners in the conversation, it ought to be seen as impertinent, inappropriate and self-serving. When women alone talk about women and religion, it is impossible for men to be transformed by new insights. When Muslim or Christian women (one could extend this to other religious groups) talk mostly within their own community of faith, or simply read the other from documents rather than in conversations and joint actions, they can easily caricature the other and miss many insights. So women must be more involved in inter-religious dialogue, for the sake of human and global transformation.

THE CHALLENGE OF GENDER DIVERSITY

Medical and psychological developments in the contemporary world have thrown up new insights into what it means to be human. This has led people into areas and possibilities that were formerly regarded as bizarre or taboo or were simply unimagined. For example, a few individuals now have sex-change operations, arguing that they have always known that they were essentially one gender though trapped in the body of the other. Such developments are new, but should not blind us to the fact that issues of sex and gender have long been important for religion, though not always well managed. Past ages have found sexuality to be a threatening, intoxicating and uncontrollable phenomenon that humans try to restrain but often without success. Hence, sexuality is treated in widely different ways within as well as between religions: for example, the practices of Tantric Hinduism contrast greatly with Mahatma Gandhi's self-imposed chastity in his later years.

Often, religions, at least in their mainstream forms, have had very conservative things to say about the fundamental meanings of human sexuality and their appropriate expressions. Nowadays, they seem very reluctant to take on board insights from the behavioural sciences, possibly because of the unsympathetic attitude towards religions of many of their seminal figures.

In this section, we shall look at the issue of same-sex relations as an example of the challenge that religions face in the new millennium for relevance and faithfulness to tradition.

It is easy to point to widespread mainstream religious disapproval of homosexual orientation and practice. The monotheistic Semitic religions certainly condemn them, but not so definitely as some assert. Scriptural texts against same-sex relations are far fewer than those that condemn injustice, slander, double standards and other commonplace human failings. In India and China, male and female homosexuality has sometimes been tolerated. In certain expressions of faith, as in classical Greece, homosexuality is viewed as a kind of rite of passage.[33] Acceptance or condemnation of homosexuality does not simply depend upon beliefs about Transcendence and her views on the subject. Societal demands are paramount: if the group needs to survive, the waste of male sperm in masturbation or homosexuality is likely to be viewed by a majority of people as anti-social, sometimes despite their own inclinations and practices. In modern societies where birth control is widely available, it is hardly surprising that few people would condemn same-sex relations on the grounds that more children are needed. It may be the case that religions have tended to impute to Transcendent reality views that derive from social and other factors and are much less justifiable than many adherents imagine to be the case.

Some justification or at least tolerance of homosexuality is located even in religions that are usually regarded as hostile to it. There are grounds for believing that same-sex relations were to some extent permitted and sometimes even cherished by the churches in Europe until the late medieval period, when fanatic and intolerant attitudes set in.[34] Medieval Muslim attitudes towards homosexuality were also sometimes more relaxed than is admitted: the obvious homo-erotic overtones of the poetry of the great Jalal al-Din Rumi (1207–1273), the mentor of the *mawlawiyya* order of 'whirling dervishes', is often overlooked by his commentators;[35] and many tales in the *Arabian Nights* are explicitly and joyfully homosexual. To be sure, these tales hardly represent the teaching of mainstream Islam; however, they are stories from medieval societies that were guided by Muslim beliefs and practices yet still managed to interpret same-sex relations in a variety of ways, some abusive but others not.[36]

To a large extent, positive assessments of same-sex relations can be construed from the same line of reasoning that justifies a more appropriate treatment of women's issues. So a case can be made that as religions struggle for relevance in a globalizing world, they will have to develop in ways that accept and rejoice in not only gender equality but also sexual diversity. One can hope that just as religions once accepted slavery, almost unthinkingly, though now this is regarded as wholly intolerable, so, in years to come, condemnatory attitudes towards homosexuality will be seen as derived more from ignorance than from knowledge and as unfair to Transcendence and to gay people. One characteristic religious approach to gay people, that their 'feelings' should be accepted but not expressed, implies little positive about an Ultimate Reality that would throw up such creations, then accept them as they are only so long as they remain celibate. This is to reduce a way of being human to the expression or otherwise of genital activity.

A major difference between the struggle for gender equality and transformed attitudes to sexual diversity is that, whereas a start has been made in altering traditional religious attitudes to the role of women, nothing comparable has been initiated in changing ways of thinking about homosexuality. It is not surprising that such reflection that has taken place has been within the Western Christian tradition and some mainly North American Jewish groups, located as they are within cultures where the movement for gay rights has been vociferous. Even within Western Christian faith, although a small amount of fascinating though speculative psychological work has been done about Jesus and his family, it is marginal to much contemporary Jesus studies and has not widely impacted upon wider Christian thought. Still, it is worth briefly surveying what has been suggested.

Jesus' father Joseph seems absent from Jesus' adult life, so he probably died before Jesus left home to follow John the Baptizer and then branch out on his own itinerant ministry. (Or else Joseph could have divorced Mary; if so, perhaps this was responsible for Jesus' vehement condemnation of divorce.[37]) Was Jesus' description of God as the ideal father forged out of his own unresolved relationship with his own father, which ended abruptly? Maybe out of the context of his own dysfunctional family, Jesus may have forged some of his central teaching about God and his kingdom. All this is highly speculative, but it is not foolishly so. From our vantage point, after the psychological insights of Sigmund Freud and Carl Jung, it is possible to interpret even ancient material with tools not previously accessible.

Some have gone further to speculate about Jesus' sexuality and his sexual orientation. His capacity to touch, heal and empathize cannot cohere with any notion of him as pale, bloodless and asexual. It is impossible to know if Jesus was celibate or married or even a widower by the time of his teaching and preaching career. If he was celibate, that need not indicate that he was gay. His relationships with both men and women do not indicate a sexual preference for one or the other or, indeed, both. It has sometimes been asserted that his friendship for the 'beloved disciple' (John 13:23) was homosexual in nature and even practice, but in many societies, affectionate and touching (in both senses of the word) male friendships do not betoken physical passion.

It is just possible that passages in the *Secret Gospel of Mark* imply that Jesus inducted his male disciples in a homosexual initiation rite. The only known fragment from this work is a quotation in a letter of Clement of Alexandria (died 215), a copy of which was discovered in 1958 by Morton Smith in the Mar Saba monastery, twelve miles southeast of Jerusalem. Some scholars doubt its authenticity, but others do not.[38] The New Testament scholar John Crossan believes it to be an early version of Mark's Gospel, dating from the early 70s.[39] At any rate, it contains a story close to John's account of the raising of Lazarus. Jesus raises from death the brother of a woman of Bethany. The young man was in the tomb. Jesus went in and revived him by grasping his hand. The text records that they went to the home of the young man, who was rich. There is an addition to the story in the *Secret Gospel of Mark* which has no parallel in John's Gospel:

> And the young man, looking at Jesus, loved and began to beseech him that he might be with him … And after six days Jesus gave him an order; and when the evening had come, the young man went to him, dressed with a linen cloth over his naked body. And he remained with him that night, because Jesus taught him the mystery of the kingdom of God.[40]

Morton Smith argues that this was a secret baptismal rite, illustrating an early libertarian as opposed to legalistic strain within Christian faith and practice. He draws attention to Paul's baptismal language, which he interprets as a ritual for union with Jesus. Although baptism was widely practised in the ancient world, Smith believes that this concept of union with Jesus is unusual and must have come from Jesus himself. He believes that 'by unknown ceremonies' the mystery of the kingdom of God was administered in water baptism by Jesus, and the disciple was possessed by Jesus's spirit and united with him. He comments that

> Freedom from the law may have resulted in completion of the spiritual union by physical union. This certainly occurred in many forms of gnostic Christianity; how early it began there is no telling.

The reader is left to infer that homosexual practices in baptismal initiation can be traced to Jesus himself and were adopted by some later Christians.[41]

Understandably, many religious people think it shocking, prurient or at least improper to discuss the sexual preferences of a great hero of faith. Perhaps a more astute judgement is that we have no means of knowing the truth of this matter. Nor is it particularly important that Jesus did not mention homosexuality, in either condemnation or affirmation. He failed to talk about (or at least to persuade others to record his thoughts on) many subjects, and arguing from silence is rarely a useful or worthy endeavour.

Perhaps there is a more credible implicit reference to Jesus' attitude towards human sexual orientation than the lubricious implications of Morton Smith's theory. He healed the Roman centurion's servant (Matthew 8:5–13; Luke 7:1–10). It has been argued that it would have been common gossip that such relationships were sexual. But the text does not afford information on this point, even though it is willing to concede the offensive enough fact (to some) that Jesus would heal the servant of an agent of foreign oppression. Even if the centurion and his servant were lovers, Jesus' act would not necessarily show that he condoned their relationship. The Gospels often, indeed usually, portray Jesus dealing with wounded, frail, imperfect humans in deep need; he had no need to heal the whole and the holy (Mark 2:17; Matthew 9:12ff.; Luke 5:31ff.).

How such interpretations of Jesus will develop in contemporary Christian theology will be fascinating to see. That they will do is certain. Christianity has understood the occasional need for an *aggiornamento*, an updating of beliefs to speak meaningfully to new contexts. In this, it is similar to other religions. Can this necessary modernization be done interfaith and dialogically? Official spokespeople for the religions seem to be unwilling to deal with the issue of homosexuality in fresh ways.

There are plenty of inter-religious meetings on marriage and the family, but most avoid the topic of same-sex relations. Many religions feel the need to shore up their commitment to the ideal of marriage and the family conceived in very conventional ways, and may even present religion as the answer to the rising tide of immorality. Some of the most fervent defenders of the 'straight' point of view at such gatherings are ascetics and celibates. For them, the choice of sexual preference is well established in their religion, whether they be, for example, Buddhist nuns or Jain monks. Religions need to consider whether, in the contemporary world, such choices need to be widened. We may query the details of modern psychological theories about human sexuality, but we disregard them only at our peril and at the cost of marginalizing people in the name of outdated assumptions. Some of the most creative artists and musicians have been gay, and have contributed greatly to Christian aesthetics, much influencing believers by their work: Leonardo da Vinci and the *Madonna Litta*, Tchaikovsky and his liturgical music are examples of this. Moreover, any sensible reading of human nature would indicate that they achieved what they did because of who they were, not despite it. Their skills were expressions of their way of being human: wonderfully creative ways, to be sure.

A beginning could be made in exploring this delicate issue at an inter-religious level by examining the attitude of foundational religious figures or religious texts to marriage and the family. After all, this seems a safe topic. Yet our survey of Jesus' attitudes recorded above suggests that such heroes may be less defenders of conventional family life than many of their followers have thought.[42] Other such icons are equally problematic. The Prophet Muhammad married about eleven times, maybe more, and had at least one important concubine. His frank admiration of the beauty of his cousin Zaynab bint Jahsh, her divorce from Muhammad's adopted son Zayd and marriage to him, sanctioned by a Qur'anic revelation, has received the disapproval of many non-Muslim scholars and even embarrassed some Muslims.[43] Siddhartha Gautama left behind his wife and baby son so that he could become the Buddha, the 'enlightened one' for humanity. All Buddhist traditions agree that it was compassion for humanity that made him do this; it was an act of supreme renunciation.[44] Maybe so; but the story fails to uphold the supreme importance of family life. Perhaps an inter-religious discussion on seminal religious figures, or crucial scriptural texts, would enable us to glean insights about ways in which our conventional notions about the right ordering of society's institutions were hardly their concern. If we undertake such an inter-religious discussion, we may be open to being more sympathetic to alternative lifestyles that regard conventional beliefs and practices as less important than truly religious goals of justice, peace and integrity.

CARE FOR CREATION

I pointed out in *Religion: A Beginner's Guide* that, although some religions are agnostic about a future life, many faith-full people believe in a life beyond, and live a life that, in their view, fits them to attain it.[45] Even those religions that are sceptical about individual post-mortem existence still believe that there is more to life than meets the eye. Nowadays, many secular people are sceptical about the attitude of many mainstream religions towards the created world, perhaps because they believe that religious men and women underestimate the value of this world and our life upon it. Although there are some believers in many faiths who, looking for the end of this world and the ushering-in of a far better reality, devalue the meaning of this earth and the life that it sustains, they hardly form the majority of faith-full people. There is a far greater threat from the implicit beliefs about reality that many contemporary secular people hold.

Since the Enlightenment, many people in Western Europe and North America have assumed a dualistic confrontation between humans and nature. People must, with the aid of technology, wrest from the world the achievements of civilization. This has led to the depletion of natural resources and the fact of global warming which, though clearly upon us, is still denied by many people whose livelihoods depend upon actions that continue to plunder the earth's produce and threaten the future of creation.

Spokespeople for religions have often naïvely claimed that this confrontational attitude is entirely the fault of Western secularism. Although there is some justification for this, the rising pollution in cities all over the world, some in areas where religion remains a deeply important part of everyday life, is just one illustration of the fact that religiously committed people, along with others, nowadays have to square the circle of wanting improved lives and a sustainable planet.

Some mainstream religions have come in for criticism for colluding with secular dualism. Other religious people, with some justification, have attacked Christianity for such complicity. Some have done so by promoting their own faith, often in naïve and idealistic terms, as the answer to the hubris of modern science and the ineffectiveness of other religions.[46]

More convincing are arguments that primal faith traditionally culti-vated a living relationship between humans and Mother Earth, which we lose at our peril. This is spelt out in the widely known testimony of Chief Seattle. He lived from 1787 to 1866, and, in his speech handing over the land of his people to the Federal Government in Washington in 1854, he spoke prophetic words about the negative results of its exploitation:

> This we know: The earth does not belong to man; man belongs to the earth. This we know. Whatever befalls the earth befalls the sons of the earth. Man did not weave the web of life; he is merely a strand in it. Whatever he does to the web he does to himself. Even the white man cannot be exempt from the common destiny. One thing we know, which the white man may one day discover – our god is the same god. You may think that you own him as you wish to own the land but you cannot. This earth is precious to the great spirit, and **to harm the earth is to heap contempt on its creator**. The whites too shall pass; perhaps sooner than all other tribes. Continue to contaminate your bed, and one night you will suffocate in your own waste.

Chief Seattle died as a Roman Catholic, with Native American customs included in his burial service. There is considerable debate about the authenticity of some or even of all his speech. As it stands, it gives the impression of being a modern creation. Still, it does seem that he said some words of prophetic and profound accuracy about the relations of people to the land they inhabit.[47]

If so, it is important not to sentimentalize them. A number of great religious figures have attempted to rescue simpler forms of life from the ravages of technological advance, but they look more eccentric than prophetic. Mahatma Gandhi's commitment to an austere life and his hopes for such ideals in an independent India are a case in point.[48] A similar naïvety is embodied in many references to the insights of primal faith. Such perspectives are moving and instructive, but they cannot easily be imposed upon the contemporary world. We are back to the underlying conviction that religious insights need to be rooted and inter-preted anew in successive generations. It is pointless to believe that we can go back to a bygone and maybe highly romanticized age. This is not to say that we cannot accept simpler lifestyles and challenge the assumptions that continuing economic growth is both possible and beneficial. It is to insist that we must work from where we are, not hunger after past possibilities.

Since most people in the world are religious, it follows that they need to be in dialogue with members of other faiths to locate their resources for a relevant and faithful commitment to ecological concerns. It is futile and self-serving to uncover idealistic options in one's own religion and compare them with a sour view of another's. If religions work together for the common good, they will also show to be false the conjecture of many secular people that some religions are inimical to ecological concerns. Many Western people who are often idealistic about Eastern and primal faiths, which they contrast favourably with the Christianity or Judaism of their origins, do not always fully appreciate the richness of the traditions they criticize. They may point out that one account of creation in Genesis tells humans to have dominion over the earth, to fill the earth and subdue it (1:26–28). Yet the whole point of this passage is that humans are to be in the image of God (1:26), to rule creation as he would, which he made to be very good. There is also an utter realism about the passage. It recognizes the fact that humans have a particularly important role within the web of life. Their knowledge and their particular relationship with Transcendent reality provide the context within which the earth will flourish or perish.

If religious people debate issues surrounding the future of the planet in an inter-religious and dialogical way, we can hope that they will be able to critique the widespread assumption of many people that, though technology has provided the problems facing the earth, it also has the solutions to them. So, for example, there are destructive weapons, but a 'Star Wars' shield can protect at least some people from them. We are removing oil from the earth, but can hope to find alternative sources of energy to resource cars, electricity and other conveniences of the modern world.

Many have reason to object to this technological optimism on the grounds of what can be called 'eco-justice'. Inner-city communities and some third world countries have become the dumping ground for toxic waste. Furthermore, when Western countries do urge other nation states not to follow their own scientific and industrial errors, it seems like denying to others what they have no intention of abandoning themselves.[49]

Religions are not simply repositories of ethical wisdom, but they are at least that. For millennia, they have helped people to live the good life. It has become fashionable for secular-minded people to condemn their fanaticism, usually without seeing the plank in their own ideology's eye when they tilt against specks elsewhere. So it would seem a matter of common sense for religions to offer their resources to a society in which many scientists and technicians have no moral basis for their actions and assumptions, or an inadequate one.

To some extent, this is already happening. A number of the global ethics project's proponents have emphasized the necessity for an ethical basis for science, which religion can help to provide.[50] Religions were also consulted in the formation of the Earth Charter, which was finally accepted after a meeting at UNESCO in Paris on 12–14 March 2000.[51] The Earth Charter Commission proposed to review responses over the following two to four years, and suggest possible amendments. Its second section focuses on 'Ecological Integrity'. It presents its principles in this section under four main headings: protect and restore the integrity of the earth's ecological systems, with special concern for biological diversity and the natural processes that sustain life; prevent harm as the best method of environmental protection and, when knowledge is limited, apply a precautionary approach; adopt patterns of production, consumption and reproduction that safeguard the Earth's regenerative capacities, human rights, and community well-being; advance the study of ecological sustainability and promote the open exchange and wide application of the knowledge acquired.[52]

The future of the planet is at a crossroads. If religions have nothing to say with a united voice, but can only defend indefensible positions or else score points off each other, they cannot hope to survive as repositories of ancient wisdom and practice.

SPIRITUALITY AND TRUTH

Religions sustain ethical views of the universe. They do so because faiths are open to a dimension of life and death that is supra-mundane, that impinges on this world and calls humans to a life of justice, truthfulness and peace.

Proponents of inter-religious dialogue contend that this dimension, to which humans have been open and in which they have believed since their earliest days on Earth,[53] is a repository of ancient wisdom which it would be folly to dismiss as out of date and misguided.

They are opposed from within the religions by those who claim that only a small proportion of those who have followed the religious quest have the truth. In their view, only the way of believing and practising that they follow is true and it alone must be followed. There are many intolerant and even fanatical people of faith, but there are also a goodly number whom faith liberates into seeking universal justice and who believe that Transcendent reality is impartial in its care for all.

The word 'truth' is a notoriously slippery one, with a variety of meanings. It does not simply convey the idea of factual accuracy, as many influenced by contemporary perspectives assume, but also communicates the virtues of integrity and vision and delineates an attitude of action not just reflection. In the contemporary world the idea of truth is often domesticated and individualized, so that you have your truth and I have mine. Although there are practitioners of dialogue who hold to this meaning, in reality it is a kind of intellectual suicide, foolishly bringing to an end long-held human convictions that wisdom is gained from the accumulated and sifted insights of many individuals and communities, past and present.

One extraordinarily powerful attempt to define truth has been made by Wilfred Cantwell Smith. Four convictions about it emerge from his work. First, *existential* truth is when participants in a religion find that the commitment that it mediates rings true for them. Second, *moral* truth is when they believe that their truth coheres with the will of Ultimate Reality. *Prepositional* truth is the truth of beliefs if and when they concur with reality and experience. Finally, God or Transcendent reality, however defined by its adherents, is the Truth from which all other truth is derived.[54]

Perhaps we should affirm that truth is a quest upon which we are all engaged and which we, as yet, grasp only provisionally. If Smith's last insight into truth is correct, as I believe it to be, it would be even better to contend that truth grasps and holds us in its grip, leading us further into truth as we live life in its presence and by its power. Anybody who has been engaged in inter-religious dialogue will know that faiths often have radically different questions and answers to the problems of life and death. It is possible to argue that these dissimilarities are more apparent than real, being culturally conditioned responses to what is essentially the same Transcendent reality as it impinges upon human beings. Sceptics of this optimistic and pluralistic view need not tread an exclusive path. They may believe that, though there are fundamentally different apprehensions of ultimate truth, which lead to quite different beliefs and practices, there is much common ground as well as areas of disagreement. Acknowledging the disagreements can help people contemplate other possibilities; we may even change our minds about certain things.

Some mystics have believed that despite our doctrinal and other differences, we nevertheless meet in the cave of the heart. It may well be that future interfaith dialogue will have much to say about appropriate spiritualities to help humans apprehend the Eternal and to respond joyfully and positively to its ways upon earth.

Such spiritualities could be particularly interesting because they enable minority and relatively powerless groups to participate in the resources of Ultimate Reality in forms that cannot easily be controlled by dominant groups. Precisely because women have often been excluded from positions of real authority in religious institutions, many of them have gained prestige and veneration in other sacred contexts. For example, many have been impressive mystics, gathering around them devotees, both men and women. The suspicion of mysticism by many people often arises out of fear that they cannot control, regulate or tame it. No wonder, then, that many men in positions of religious authority are often particularly disapproving of mysticism. Although there is a right and proper respect for authority figures and institutions in religions, such figures and institutions do not exhaust the variety of ways of being religious.[55] Mysticism is not a less genuine and integral part of religious experience because many faith-full people are puzzled by or wary of it. Neither do authoritative institutions completely define and control religions. For example, whatever the importance of the institution of the papacy in the Roman Catholic Church, it does not exhaust the meaning of that church nor is it the sole source of power, though some popes have claimed otherwise.

Religion is neither a monarchy nor a democracy. It can be the tool of dictators and megalomaniacs, or captured and misunderstood by the abused and the cruel. In truth, though, it is a phenomenon that points us beyond the narrow horizons of our sentient life, boundaried by sensory experiences and language, to tap into a Transcendent reality that has transformative possibilities for us all. From earliest times, humans have believed that there is meaning to life, not imparted to people who are content with superficial things, but conveyed to those who have faith. Faith is not wishful thinking. It is trust, verified in the relationship we have with that ultimate vision and how it sustains and shapes our living and our dying.

The present time of rapid globalization, with both its good and its evil consequences, surely commits us to inter-religious dialogue. People of particular religions must move on from simply accepting and rejoicing that Transcendence reveals herself only to them and those who are like them. If God speaks to us and, it would seem, from their testimony, to others too, we must seek to understand what Ultimate Reality has to disclose through others who also claim to hear his voice. Our dialogue with other people is the respectful attention we offer to those who are also included within the scope of eternal, revelatory grace. As we listen, we will have things to teach and learn from each other, sharing disclosures from a wisdom that is beyond us yet breaks into our lives. In our continuing dialogue, we can hope to grow further into the Truth that offers healing or salvation to our wounded world, which, for all its troubles, most humans in most times and places have believed to be brooded over by an eternal Spirit of transforming grace.

NOTES

CHAPTER 1

1. For an overview of the early days of the interfaith scene in the United Kingdom, see my article in Forward et al., 2000, pp. 33–44; and also my reflections towards the end of this chapter.
2. Mar Gregorios, 1992, pp. 9–14.
3. Wittgenstein, 1963, 31ff., 66ff.
4. Forward, 2001, Chapter 1.
5. Whitehead, 1929, p. 63.
6. e.g. Vermes, 1993, p. 214.
7. Sanders, 1991, p. 118ff.
8. Hodgson, 1974, p. 80.
9. Anon., 1988, p. 55ff.
10. Forward et al., 2000.
11. Anon., 1988, p. 51.
12. Glubb, 1970, p. 9.
13. French, 1994.
14. Braybrooke, 1996, *passim*.
15. Quoted in Cragg, 1992, p. 18.
16. Quoted in Cragg, 1992, p. 17.
17. Quoted in Padwick, 1953, p. 171ff.

CHAPTER 2

1. Toynbee, 1948–1961, *passim*.
2. It is the subject matter of his book, 1970.
3. Hick, 1983, p. 82.
4. Liechty, 1990, p. 86.
5. Parrinder, 1987, p. 224.
6. DiNoia, 1992, p. ix.

7. Hick, 1995, pp. 17, 21.
8. English, 1994, p. 161.
9. See, e.g., Lesslie Newbigin's summary in Wainwright, 1989, pp. 331–333.
10. e.g. Forward, 1998b, especially Chapter 3.
11. Forward, 1995, pp. 113, 114ff.
12. Ware, 1993, pp. 123, 181, 188ff.
13. Cracknell, 1995, *passim.*
14. See an intriguing book on what lies beyond death, according to the world's religions, edited by a Jew and a Christian: Cohn-Sherbok and Lewis, 1995, *passim.* Even here, however, most contributors are Christians, some of whom write (usually very insightfully) about other positions than their own.
15. Huxley, 1946, *passim.*
16. Huxley, 1946, p. 1
17. For a more detailed critique of the perennial philosophy, see Forward, 2001, Chapter 1.
18. Forward et al., 2000, pp. 61–75.
19. Curnock, 1938, vol. 1, p. 345ff.
20. Curnock, 1938, vol. 1, p. 367.
21. Curnock, 1938, vol. 2, p. 63.
22. Curnock, 1938, vol. 5, p. 354.
23. Outler, 1985, p. 486.
24. Outler, 1986, pp. 493, 496.
25. Outler, 1986, p. 491.
26. Outler, 1986, p. 494ff.
27. Outler, 1986, p. 500.
28. After his conversion experience in May 1738, Wesley saw pre-justification good works as 'splendid sins', remarkable and edifying but still transgressions. By 1744 he had changed his mind, and recognized a place for human ignorance about God.
29. Quoted in Forward, 1998b, p. 48.
30. Wesley, 1950, p. 434ff.
31. Turner, 1985, p. 47.
32. Dinshaw and Steel, 1986, p. 150.
33. Green and Gollancz, 1962, p. 147ff.
34. Küng, 1996, pp. 12–26.
35. The issue of religion and women is dealt with at greater length in Chapter 5.
36. Zeldin, 1998, p. 18ff.
37. Fackenheim, 1994, p. xixf.
38. Berthrong, 1999, *passim.*
39. Mayer, 1991, p. 34.
40. The variant forms of this universal rule are set out especially well in Fisher, 1999, p. 104.
41. Montefiore and Loewe, 1974, pp. 173, 200.

CHAPTER 3

1. Parrinder, 1953, Chapters 2 and 3.
2. Bowie with Deacy, 1997, p. 208.
3. An early, brilliant and rather neglected book by a distinguished historian which foreshadowed many others is Barraclough, 1964.
4. e.g. Surin in D'Costa, 1990, pp. 192–212.
5. See the excellent article by Paul Knitter in D'Arcy May, 1998, pp. 75–89.
6. See the discussion in Forward, 2000, Chapter 1.
7. Lindbeck, 1984, *passim*.
8. Forward, 1998b, pp. 95–146.
9. Smith, 1981, *passim*.
10. e.g. Panikkar, 1999, *passim*.
11. Meadows, 1996, p. 39.
12. Meadows, 1996, p. 35.
13. 'Infect' is rather a strong word. See e.g. Wiebe, 1999, p. 153.
14. Wiebe, 1999, *passim*.
15. McCutcheon, 1997, *passim*.
16. This is discussed further in Forward, 2000, Chapter 1.
17. Forward, 2000, Introduction.
18. Bowker, 1995, p. 181ff.
19. Bowker, 1995, p. ix.
20. Bowker, 1995, p. x.
21. Bowker, 1985, p. xi.
22. Hillberg, 1985, p. 10ff.
23. This story is recounted in Cracknell, 1986: p. 119f.
24. Lochhead, 1988, provides a good example of this claim.
25. Green, 1999, pp. 157–166.
26. See McCutcheon, 1999, *passim*.
27. Smart, 1995, pp. 7–10.
28. These are its various meanings in the Greek New Testament.
29. e.g. O'Dea, 1957.
30. Cracknell, 1995, the title of his book.

CHAPTER 4

1. Cohn-Sherbok, 1992, p. 104.
2. Braybrooke, 1991, p. 14.
3. Braybrooke, 1991, p. 15ff.
4. Roth, 1978, pp. 85–88, 164–166, 259–270.
5. Parrinder, 1987, p. 120ff.
6. Braybrooke, 1991, p. 3.
7. Parkes, 1969, *passim*.
8. Christie, 1935, pp. 19, 21.
9. Christie, 1977, p. 465ff.
10. Barnard, 1980, p. 24.

11. Braybrooke, 1991, p. 34
12. The text can be found on the website: www.vatican.va, in the section 'The Roman Curia'. The teaching that other world religions result from a purely human quest for God is found on page 7.
13. An enthusiastic though not very self-critical account of the making of *Nostra Aetate* is that of: Oesterreicher, 1986, *passim*.
14. This Christian depiction of Jews is brilliantly illustrated in: Schreckenberg, 1996: *passim*.
15. Wigoder, 1988, pp. 77–81.
16. Cornwell, 1999, *passim*.
17. The best source of up-to-date information about Roman Catholic, Protestant and Jewish documents, which seem to be added to almost on a daily basis, is the website www.jcrelations.net
18. Karl Barth's ambivalent attitude to the Jews and his appraisal of them from a naïve and negative Christian theological stance are well illustrated by Haynes, 1995, Chapter 4.
19. The Methodist Conference 1994 Agenda, p. 592.
20. The Methodist Conference 1994 Agenda, p. 593.
21. www.jcrelations.net
22. The text of *Dabru Emet* and commentary upon it can be found in www.jcrelations.net
23. Klein, 1978, *passim*.
24. Ruether, 1997, p. 246.
25. Sanders, 1992, p. 494.
26. Sanders, 1985, especially pp. 321–327.
27. Vermes, 1993, p. 214.
28. Forward, 1999, p. 58ff.
29. Vermes, 1998, *passim*.
30. e.g. Rahman, 1979, p. 32ff.
31. The website of CJCR is www.cjcr.org
32. Fackenheim, 1970, pp. 67–98; 1994, p. xixf.
33. Braybrooke, 1991, p. 30.
34. Birkland, 1987, *passim*.
35. e.g. Werblowsky, 1978, *passim*.
36. Ucko, 1996, *passim*.
37. Watt 1991, p. 107
38. Said 1985, p. 300ff.
39. Carrier, 1995: *passim*.
40. e.g. Tambiah, 1992: *passim*.
41. Eck, 1993, p. 59.
42. Schwartz, 1997, p. x.
43. Such work already has promising beginnings. See, for example, Hilton with Marshall, 1988, *passim*; Forward, in Phan, 1990, pp. 103–115.
44. Southern, 1962, *passim*. Daniel, 1993, *passim*.
45. Edwards, 2000.

CHAPTER 5

1. For a fuller discussion of religions as boundaried systems, see the section on 'Dialogue: a definition' in Chapter 1 of this book; and also Chapter 1 of my *Religion: A Beginner's Guide*.
2. Berthrong, 1999, *passim*.
3. See Forward, 1995, p. 167. Lipner describes himself there as a 'Hindu-Catholic'.
4. Forward, 1995, p. 113.
5. Ariarajah, 1999, p. 4.
6. Forward, 1995, p. 24.
7. See also Julius Lipner in Forward, 1995, pp. 167–175.
8. Cracknell, 2001, *passim*.
9. Cazden, 1983, pp. 73–84.
10. D'Arcy May, 1998, p. 46.
11. Cazden, 1983, p. 233.
12. Sheridan, 1994, p. ix-xiv.
13. Forward, 1999, p. 63.
14. Warner, 1978, *passim*.
15. D'Arcy May, 1998, p. 51.
16. *Methodist Worship Book*, 1999, p. 204.
17. Imagery of God in the Qur'an is overwhelmingly masculine. But see Schimmel, 1997, *passim*.
18. Haddon, 1910, p. 79.
19. Garnsey, 1996, pp. 80–85, 240–243.
20. Bamyeh, 2000, *passim*.
21. Ahmed, 1992, *passim*.
22. Mernissi, 1985, p. 19.
23. Ali, 1922, p. 230.
24. Mernissi, 1991a, p. 85ff, 162ff.
25. Mernissi, 1991a, p. 104.
26. Mernissi 1991b, p. 72–79.
27. Ameer Ali, 1922, p. 296.
28. Harris, 1998, p. 132ff.
29. D'Arcy May, 1998, p. 52.
30. e.g. Wren, 1989, *passim*. Pryce, 1997, *passim*.
31. Daly, 1986, p. 3.
32. Daly, 1978, pp. 107–312.
33. Parrinder, 1995, pp. 21, 99, 204.
34. Boswell, 1980, p. 269.
35. Forward, 1997, pp. 47–49.
36. Irwin, 1994, pp. 168–171.
37. Jesus seems to have forbidden divorce. Its prohibition appears once in Paul's writings (1 Corinthians 7:10ff.) and four times in the Synoptic Gospels (Mark 10:2–12; Matthew 5:31ff., 19:3–9; Luke 16:18). The Gospels have a long form (Mark and Matthew 19) and a short form

(Matthew 5 and Luke); Paul's account is nearer to the short form. It is impossible to know which is more authentic. The short form more or less condemns remarriage of divorced people as adultery. The longer form has Jesus argue that marriage is an act of creation and that Moses permitted divorce only because of the hardness of human hearts. At any rate, like the shorter form, it forbids divorced people to marry again.

38. Koester, 1990, pp. 293–303.
39. Crossan, 1991, p. 429ff.
40. Koester, 1990, p. 296.
41. Smith, 1973, p. 97–114.
42. Forward, 1998b, Chapter 3.
43. Forward, 1997, pp. 83–88.
44. Harris, 1998, p. 16.
45. Forward, 2001, Chapter 4.
46. See, for example, Nasr, 1976, *passim*.
47. For the speech and discussions about it, including its authenticity, visit www.dimensional.com/~randl/seatbib.htm
48. Brown, 1989, p. 89ff.
49. Berthrong, 1999, pp. 118–120.
50. Küng, 1996, p. 37ff.
51. Berthrong, 1999, pp. 126–130.
52. www.earthcharter.org
53. Forward, 2001, Chapter 1.
54. Vroom, 1989, p. 80ff.
55. Forward, 2001, Chapter 3.

BIBLIOGRAPHY

Ahmed, L., *Women and Gender in Islam*. New Haven and London, Yale University Press, 1992.

Ameer Ali, S., *The Spirit of Islam* (rev. edn). London, Christophers, 1922.

Anon., *Sri Sarada Devi*. Calcutta, Advaita Ashrama, 1988.

Ariarajah, S.W., *Not Without My Neighbour: Issues in Interfaith Relations*. Geneva, WCC 1999.

Bamyeh, M., *The Social Origins of Islam*. St Paul's, University of Minnesota Press, 2000.

Banfield. S., *Gerald Finzi*. London and Boston, Faber & Faber, 1997.

Barker, E. (ed.), *New Religious Movements: A Practical Introduction*. London, HMSO, 1989.

Barnard, R., *A Talent to Deceive. An Appreciation of Agatha Christie*. London, Collins, 1980.

Barraclough, G., *An Introduction to Contemporary History*. London, C.A. Watts, 1964.

Berthrong, J., *The Divine Deli*. Maryknoll, Orbis, 1999.

Bevan Jones, L., *The People of the Mosque*. Calcutta, Baptist Missionary Press, 1965.

Birkland, C.J. (ed.), *Unified in Hope. Arabs and Jews Talk about Peace*. Geneva, WCC, 1987.

Boswell, J., *Christianity, Social Tolerance, and Homosexuality. Gay People in Western Europe from the Beginning of the Christian Era to the Fourteenth Century*. Chicago and London, Chicago University Press, 1980.

Bowie, F. with Deacy, C. (eds.), *The Coming Deliverer: Millennial Themes in World Religions*. Cardiff, University of Wales Press, 1997.

Bowker, J., *Licensed Insanities*. London, Darton Longman & Todd, 1987.

Bowker, J., *The Sense of God*. Oxford, Oneworld, 1995.

Braybrooke, M., *Children of One God. A History of the Council of Christians and Jews*. London, Valentine Mitchell, 1991.

Braybrooke, M., *A Wider Vision: A History of the World Congress of Faiths*. Oxford, Oneworld, 1996.

Brown, J.M., *Gandhi. Prisoner of Hope*. New Haven and London, Yale University Press, 1989.

Carrier, J.G. (ed.), *Occidentalism*. Oxford, Oxford University Press, 1995.

Cazden, E., *Antoinette Brown Blackwell. A Biography*. New York, Feminist Press, 1983.

Christie, A., *Three Act Tragedy*. London, Fontana, 1935.

Christie, A., *An Autobiography*. London, Collins, 1977.

Cohn-Sherbok, D. (ed.), *Many Mansions*. London, Bellew, 1992.

Cohn-Sherbok, D. and Lewis, C. (eds.), *Beyond Death*. London, Macmillan, 1995.

Cornford, F.M., *The Republic of Plato*. Oxford, Oxford University Press, 1945.

Cornwell, J., *Hitler's Pope*. New York and London, Viking, 1999.

Cracknell, K., *Towards a New Relationship*. London, Epworth, 1986.

Cracknell, K., *Justice, Courtesy and Love. Theologians and Missionaries Encountering World Religions 1846–1914*. London, Epworth, 1995.

Cracknell, K., *Wilfred Cantwell Smith: A Reader*. Oxford, Oneworld, 2001.

Cragg, K., *Troubled by Truth*. Durham, Pentland Press, 1992.

Crossan, J.D., *The Historical Jesus. The Life of a Mediterranean Jewish Peasant*. Edinburgh, T & T Clark, 1991.

Curnock, N. (ed.), *The Journal of the Rev. John Wesley, A.M. Volumes 1, 2, 5*. London, Epworth, 1938.

Daly, M., *Gyn/Ecology. The Metaethics of Radical Feminism*. Boston, Beacon Press, 1978.

Daly, M., *Beyond God the Father*. London, Women's Press, 1986.

Daniel, N., *Islam and the West*. Oxford, Oneworld, 1993.

D'Arcy May, J. (ed.), *Pluralism and the Religions*. London, Cassell, 1998.

D'Costa, G. (ed.), *Christian Uniqueness Reconsidered*. Maryknoll, Orbis, 1990.

DiNoia, J., *The Diversity of Religions*. Washington, Catholic University of America, 1992.

Dinshaw, N. and Steel, D. (eds.), *The Liberal Heart*. London, Firethorn Press, 1986.

Eck, D., *Encountering God*. Boston, Beacon Press, 1993.

Edwards, M. (ed.), *Words for Today 2000*. Birmingham, IBRA, 2000.

English, D. (ed.), *Windows on Salvation*. London, Darton Longman & Todd, 1994.

Ericksen, R.P., *Theologians under Hitler*. New Haven and London, Yale University Press, 1985.

Fackenheim, E., *God's Presence in History*. New York, New York University 1970.

Fackenheim, E., *To Mend the World*. Bloomington and Indianapolis, Indiana University Press, 1994.

Fisher, M.P., *Religion in the Twenty-First Century*. London, Routledge, 1999.

Forward, M. (ed.), *Ultimate Visions*. Oxford, Oneworld, 1995.

Forward, M., *Muhammad: A Short Biography*. Oxford, Oneworld, 1997.

Forward, M., *A Bag of Needments. Geoffrey Parrinder and the Study of Religion*. Bern, Peter Lang, 1998a.

Forward, M., *Jesus: A Short Biography*. Oxford, Oneworld, 1998b.

Forward, M., *The Failure of Islamic Modernism? Syed Ameer Ali's Interpretation of Islam as a Religion*. Bern, Peter Lang, 1999.

Forward, M., *Religion: A Beginner's Guide*. Oxford, Oneworld, 2001.

Forward, M., Plant, S., and White, S., *A Great Commission*. Bern, Peter Lang, 2000.

French, P., *Younghusband: The Last Great Imperial Adventurer*. London, HarperCollins, 1994.

Garnsey, P., *Ideas of Slavery from Aristotle to Augustine*. Cambridge, Cambridge University Press, 1996.

Glubb, J., *The Life and Times of Muhammad*. New York, Scarborough House, 1970.

Green, B. and Gollancz, V. (eds.), *God of a Hundred Names*. London, Victor Gollancz, 1962.

Green, G., *Theology, Hermeneutics and Imagination*. Cambridge, Cambridge University Press, 1999.

Haddon, A.C., *History of Anthropology*. London and New York, Knickerbocker Press, 1910.

Harris, E., *What Buddhists Believe*. Oxford, Oneworld, 1998.

Haynes, S.R., *Jews and the Christian Imagination*. London, Macmillan, 1995.

Heim, S.M. (ed.), *Grounds for Understanding*. Grand Rapids and Cambridge, Eerdman, 1998.

Hick, J., *The Second Christianity*. London, SCM, 1983.

Hick, J., *The Rainbow of Faiths*. London, SCM, 1995.

Hillberg, R., *The Destruction of the European Jews*. London and New York, Holmes & Meier, 1985.

Hilton, M. with Marshall, G., *The Gospels and Rabbinic Judaism. A Study Guide*. London, SCM, 1988.

Hodgson, M., *The Venture of Islam, 3. The Gunpowder Empires and Modern Times*. Chicago and London, University of Chicago Press, 1974.

Huxley, A., *The Perennial Philosophy*. London, Chatto & Windus, 1946.

Irwin, R., *The Arabian Nights: A Companion*. London and New York, Allen Lane, 1994.

Klein, C., *Anti-Judaism in Christian Theology*. London, SPCK, 1978.

Koester, H., *Ancient Christian Gospels*. London, SCM, 1990.

Kuhn, T., *The Structure of Scientific Revolutions*, 2nd edn. Chicago, University of Chicago Press, 1970.

Küng, H., *Yes to a Global Ethic*. London, SCM, 1996.

Liechty, D., *Theology in Postliberal Perspective*. London, SCM, 1990.

Lindbeck, G.A., *The Nature of Doctrine*. Philadelphia, Westminster Press, 1984.

Lockhead, D., *The Dialogical Imperative*. New York, Orbis, 1988.

Mar Gregorios, P., *A Light Too Bright. The Enlightenment Today*. Albany, State University of New York Press, 1963.

Maybaum, I., *The Face of God after Auschwitz*. Amsterdam, Polak & Van Gennep, 1965.

Mayer, A.E., *Islam and Human Rights*. London, Pinter, 1991.

McCutcheon, R.T., *Manufacturing Religion*. New York and Oxford, Oxford University Press, 1997.

McCutcheon, R.T., *The Insider/Outsider Problem in the Study of Religion*. London and New York, Cassell, 1999.

McPherran, M.L., *The Religion of Socrates*. University Park, PA, Penn State Press, 1999.

Meadows, P., 'Virtual Insidership: Interreligious Dialogue and the Limits of Understanding', *Discernment*, 3(2) 1996, pp.29–41.

Mehta, G., *Karma Cola. Marketing the Mystic East*. London, Jonathan Cape, 1980.

Mernissi, F., *Beyond the Veil*. London, Ali Saqi, 1985.

Mernissi, F., *The Veil and the Male Élite*. Reading, Addison-Wesley, 1991a.

Mernissi, F., *Women and Islam*. Oxford, Blackwell, 1991b.

Mernissi, F., *The Harem within. Tales of a Moroccan Childhood*. New York and London, Bantam, 1995.

Methodist Worship Book. Peterborough, Methodist Publishing House, 1999.

Montefiore, C.G. and Loewe, H., *A Rabbinic Anthology*. New York, Schocken, 1974.

Morton, R., *One Island Many Faiths. The Experience of Religions in Britain*. London, Thames & Hudson, 2000.

Nasr, S.H., *Islamic Science: An Illustrated Study*. London, World of Islam, 1976.

O'Dea, T.F., *The Mormons*. Chicago, Phoenix, 1957.

Oesterreicher, J.M., *The New Encounter between Christians and Jews*. New York, Philosophical Library, 1986.

Outler, A.C. (ed.), *The Works of John Wesley, Vol. 2*. Nashville, Abingdon, 1985.

Outler, A.C. (ed.), *The Works of John Wesley, Vol. 3*. Nashville, Abingdon, 1986

Padwick, C., *Henry Martyn: Confessor of the Faith*. London, Inter-Varsity Fellowship, 1953.

Panikkar, R., *The Intra-Religious Dialogue*. Mahwah, NJ, Paulist Press, 1999.

Parkes, J., *Voyages of Discovery*. London, Victor Gollancz, 1969.

Parrinder, G., *Religion in an African City*. Oxford, Oxford University Press, 1953.

Parrinder, G., *Encountering World Religions*. Edinburgh, T & T Clark, 1987.

Parrinder, G., *Sexual Morality in the World's Religions*. Oxford, Oneworld, 1995.

Phan, P. (ed.), *Christianity and the Wider Ecumenism*. New York, Paragon House, 1990.

Pryce, M., *Finding a Voice. Men, Women and the Community of the Church*. Harrisburg, PA, Trinity Press, 1997.

Rahman, F., *Islam*. Chicago and London, University of Chicago Press, 1979.

Roth, C., *A History of the Jews in England*. Oxford, Clarendon Press, 1978.

Ruether, R., *Faith and Fratricide*. Oregon, Wipf & Stock, 1997.

Said, E., *Orientalism*. London, Routledge & Kegan Paul, 1978.

Said, E., *Covering Islam*. New York, Pantheon, 1981.

Sanders, E.P., *Jesus and Judaism*. London, SCM, 1985.

Sanders, E.P., *Paul*. Oxford, Oxford University Press, 1991.

Sanders, E.P., *Judaism Practice and Belief 63BCE – 66CE*. London, SCM, 1992.

Schimmel, A., *My Soul Is a Woman. The Feminine in Islam*. New York, Continuum, 1997.

Schreckenberg, H., *The Jews in Christian Art*. London, SCM, 1996.

Schwartz, R.M., *The Curse of Cain*. Chicago and London, University of Chicago Press, 1997.

Seager, R.H., *The Dawn of Religious Pluralism: Voices from the World's Parliament of Religions*. 1893. La Salle, IL, Open Court, 1993.

Sheridan, S. (ed.), *Hear Our Voice. Women Rabbis Tell Their Stories*. London, SCM, 1994.

Smart, N., *Choosing a Faith*. London, Boyers/Bowerdean, 1995.

Smith, M., *The Secret Gospel. The Discovery and Interpretation of the Secret Gospel According to Mark*. London, Harper & Row, 1973.

Smith, W.C., *Towards a World Theology: Faith and the Comparative Study of Religion*. London, Macmillan, 1981.

Southern, R.W., *Western Views of Islam in the Middle Ages*. Cambridge, MA, Harvard University Press, 1962.

Stendahl, K., *Paul among Jews and Gentiles*. Philadelphia, Fortress Press, 1976.

Stuart, E. et al., *Religion Is a Queer Thing. A Guide to the Christian Faith for Lesbian, Gay, Bisexual and Transgendered People*. London, Cassell, 1997.

Tambiah, S.J., *Buddhism Betrayed? Religion, Politics, and Violence in Sri Lanka*. Chicago, Chicago University Press, 1992.

Toynbee, A.J., *A Study of History*. London, Oxford University Press, 1948–61.

Turner, J.M., *Conflict and Reconciliation: Studies in Methodism and Ecumenism in England 1740–1982*. London, Epworth, 1985.

Twiss, S.B. and Grelle, B. (eds.), *Explorations in Global Ethics: Comparative Religious Ethics and Interreligious Dialogue*. Boulder and Oxford, Westview Press, 1998.

Ucko, H. (ed.), *People of God, Peoples of God*. Geneva, WCC, 1996.

Vermes, G., *The Religion of Jesus the Jew*. London, SCM, 1993.

Vermes, G., *Providential Accidents. An Autobiography*. London, SCM, 1998.

Vroom, H.M., *Religions and the Truth*. Amsterdam and Grand Rapids, Editions Rodopi and Eerdmans, 1989.

Wainwright, G. (ed.), *Keeping the Faith*. London, SPCK, 1989.

Ware, T., *The Orthodox Church*. Harmondsworth, Penguin, 1993.

Warner, M., *Alone of All Her Sex. The Myth and the Cult of the Virgin Mary*. London and New York, Quartet, 1978.

Watt, W.M., *Muslim–Christian Encounters*. London, Routledge, 1991.

Werblowsky, R.J.Z., *The Meaning of Jerusalem to Jews, Christians and Muslims*, rev. edn. *Jerusalem*, Israel Universities' Study Group for Middle Eastern Affairs, 1978.

Wesley, J., *Explanatory Notes upon the New Testament*. London, Epworth, 1950.

Whaling, F. (ed.), *Religion in Today's World*. Edinburgh, T & T Clark, 1987.

Whitehead, A., *Process and Reality*. New York, Macmillan, 1929.

Wiebe, D., *The Politics of Religious Studies*. New York, St Martin's Press, 1999.

Wigoder, G., *Jewish–Christian Relations since the Second World War*. Manchester and New York, Manchester University Press, 1988.

Wittgenstein, L., *Philosophical Investigations*. Oxford, Blackwell, 1963.

Wren, B., *What Language Shall I Borrow?* London, SCM, 1989.

Zeldin, T., *An Intimate History of Humanity*. London, Vintage, 1998.

Ziesler, J., *Paul's Letter to the Romans*. London, SCM, 1989.

INDEX